Albert Ruger

Panoramic Maps
of Anglo-American Cities

A Checklist of Maps in the Collections of the
Library of Congress, Geography and
Map Division

Compiled by John R. Hébert

LIBRARY OF CONGRESS   WASHINGTON   1974

Cover: Hermann, Mo., 1869.   Drawn by Albert Ruger.

Library of Congress Cataloging in Publication Data

United States.   Library of Congress.   Geography
  and Map Division.
    Panoramic maps of Anglo-American cities.

    1. Cities and towns—United States—Maps—
Bibliography.   2.   Cities and towns—Canada—Maps—
Bibliography.   3.   United States.   Library of Congress.
Geography and Map Division.   I.   Hébert, John R.
II.   Title.
Z6027.U5U54 1974   016.912′7   73-18312
ISBN 0-8444-0114-5

For sale by the Superintendent of Documents, U.S. Government Printing Office
Washington, D.C. 20402–Price $2.20 cents
Stock Number 3004–00011

Preface

This checklist records 1,117 panoramic maps of Anglo-American cities which are preserved in the collections of the Library of Congress, Geography and Map Division. Manuscript and printed maps—including photocopies of originals in other repositories—of cities in 47 states, the District of Columbia, and Canada, are identified. A descriptive essay on the panormaic map industry in Victorian America precedes the entries. The general index to city names, artists, publishers, and lithographers/printers enhances the utility of the checklist. Entries are arranged alphabetically and chronologically by cities within each state. Because maps are listed by the name in the title, users are advised to consult the index to locate all maps of a particular city.

The columns in the checklist include, respectively: 1) entry number, 2) city name, 3) artists, 4) publisher, and, if noted on the map, place of publication, 5) lithographer or printer, with his location, if noted, and 6) map size. Names of artists, publishers, and lithographers are given as they appear on the maps, except that the words "and" and "Company" are consistently abbreviated "&" and "Co." Unless otherwise noted in the last column, the item recorded is a printed map. The map size is given in inches, with the vertical dimension first. Insets or side views to the main map are not always indicated in the list, and no differentiation has been made between colored and noncolored views.

Black-and-white photoreproductions of most of the maps cited in this checklist may be purchased from the Photoduplication Service, Library of Congress, Washington, D.C. 20540. The 16- by 20-inch matte finish photographic prints are recommended for decorative purposes, and glossy prints are best suited for use in publications. Maps larger than 37 by 48 inches cannot be reproduced on a single film negative, and multiple photostatic or photographic prints must be ordered. Requests for cost estimates or purchase orders should refer to the maps by title and give entry numbers. It is not possible to supply reproductions of panoramic maps for which the Library has only photocopies. Names and addresses of libraries holding originals of these items will be supplied upon request.

The Library of Congress has a large, although not complete, collection of panoramic maps. The nucleus of the collection consists of maps received by copyright deposit, but the files have also been enriched by transfers from other Federal agencies, purchases, gifts, and copies of originals in other libraries. Most of the panoramic maps, including those in this checklist, are in the Geography and Map Division, although a small number are preserved in the Library's Prints and Photographs Division. The Geography and Map Division is interested in securing originals or photocopies of panoramic maps not already in its collections and will welcome information which may lead to such acquisitions.

John R. Hébert

Contents

Panoramic Maps of Anglo-American Cities

This 1893 view of Morrisville, Pa., with insets of residences and business establishments, was commissioned by a local realtor. Drawn and published by Thaddeus M. Fowler.

Introduction

A popular cartographic form used to depict Anglo-America's cities and towns during the late 19th and early 20th centuries was the panoramic map. Known also as bird's-eye views, perspective maps, panoramas, and aero views, panoramic maps are nonphotographic representations of cities, portrayed as if viewed from above at an oblique angle. Although not generally drawn to scale, they show street patterns, individual buildings, and major landscape features in perspective.

Preparation of panoramic maps involved a vast amount of painstakingly detailed labor. For each project a frame or projection was developed, showing in perspective the pattern of streets. The artist then walked the streets, sketching buildings, trees, and other features to present a complete and accurate landscape as though seen from an elevation of 2,000 to 3,000 feet.[1] These data were entered on the frame in his workroom.

Perspective mapping was not unique to the United States and Canada or to the Victorian period. Mathias Merian, George Braun, and Franz Hogenberg, among others, produced perspective maps of European cities in the late 16th and early 17th centuries. These early European town plans, most often portraying major political or marketing centers, were small in size and were generally incorporated in atlases or geographical books. The perspective was usually at a low oblique angle, and streets were seldom identified by name. In some instances, the views were hypothetical, and one pattern might be used to represent various European cities.

A modified version of the Renaissance city view was employed in the United States before the Civil War. Like their European predecessors, these perspectives, usually of large cities, were drawn at low oblique angles and at times even at ground level. Street patterns were often indistinct. Also popular during this period were views of American cities drawn as though viewed from extremely great heights.

Victorian America's panoramic maps differ dramatically from the Renaissance city perspectives. The post-Civil War town views are more accurate and are drawn from a higher oblique angle. Small towns as well as major urban centers were portrayed. Panoramic mapping of urban centers was unique to North America in this era. Most panoramic maps were published independently, not as plates in an atlas or in a descriptive geographical book. Preparation and sale of 19th-century panoramas were motivated by civic pride and the desire of the city fathers to encourage commercial growth. Many views were prepared for and endorsed by chambers of commerce and other civic organizations and were used as advertisements of a city's commercial and residential potential.

Advances in lithography, photolithography, photoengraving, and chromolithography, which made possible inexpensive and multiple copies, coupled with a prosperous populace willing to purchase prints, made panoramic maps popular wall hangings during America's Victorian Age. The citizen could view with pride his immediate environment and point out his own property to guests, since the map artist, for a suitable fee, obligingly included illustrations of private homes as insets to the main city plan.

Real estate agents and chambers of commerce used the maps to promote sales to prospective buyers of homes and business properties. Henry Wellge's 1892 panorama of Norfolk, Va., for example, was distributed with the compliments of Pollard Brothers Real Estate, and Thaddeus M. Fowler's 1893 view of Morrisville, Pa., was commissioned by realtor William G. Howell.[2] Panoramic maps not only showed the existing city but sometimes also depicted areas planned for development. Fowler's 1890 map of Childress, Tex., and 1907 map of South Rocky Mount, N.C., are examples.

Panoramic maps graphically depict the exciting and vibrant life of a city. Harbors are shown choked with ships, often to the extent of constituting hazards to navigation. Trains speed along railroad tracks, at times on the same roadbed with locomotives and cars headed in the opposite direction. People and horsedrawn carriages fill the streets, and smoke belches from stacks of industrial plants. Urban and industrial development in post-Civil War America is vividly portrayed in the maps.

As late as the 1920's, panoramic maps were still in vogue commercially. A view of Derby, Conn., by Hughes & Bailey used on a letterhead of this period, includes a description of the various advantages the city could offer a new industry or a prospective home buyer. The promotional pitch concluded with the following observation:

The many Natural Advantages of Location, the Cheapness of Power, Varied Industries, Skilled Labor, Facilities for Transportation, Proximity to other Large Manufacturing Communities combine to make Derby Exceptionally Attractive to the Manufacturer and Home Seeker as a Commercial and an Industrial Center.[3]

Norris, Wellge & Co.'s 1885 view of Madison, Wis., illustrates another use of panoramic maps. In addition to those sold for wall hangings, copies of the view were used by S. L. Sheldon to advertise his farm implement store. The map is framed by 18 pictures of farm machines, including the Gasaday sulky plow, the J. I. Case agitator, Buffalo Pitts coal or wood burning traction engine, and Esterly's twine binding harvester. Sheldon sent copies of the panorama to his patrons, along with a request for their continued patronage. Similarly, Fowler's 1889 map of Hamburg, Pa., contains two advertisements below the neat line. One portrays W. William Appel's photographic studio, jewelry store, and residence, with a lithographic reproduction of the owner. The other, an advertisement for W. H. Grim, dealer in musical instruments and sewing machines, includes a view of his shop and a representation of a Miller organ, one of Grim's stock items.

There is little information about the number of prints usually published or the customary selling price. Obviously, more impressions were made of large city maps than of those picturing small towns. A recent estimate from Meriden Gravure Company, Meriden, Conn., the printer of Hughes & Bailey and Hughes & Cinquin aero views in the 1910's and 1920's, noted that between 100 and 250 copies of each view were generally printed.[4] However, Oakley H. Bailey, one of the bird's-eye view artists, stated in 1932 that he had made sketches of nearly 600 different places and that total reproductions had exceeded a million copies. Simple arithmetic indicates that Bailey's estimate works out to approximately 2,000 copies of each view.[5] Considering the scarcity of many views, it may be assumed that the average printing was probably in the neighborhood of 500 impressions.

The cost of the individual bird's-eye view was very likely determined by the number of impressions and the buying capability of the citizenry. The following note, appended to H. H. Bailey's 1872 view of Milwaukee, Wis., gives some help:

Our birdseye view of Milwaukee (size 26×40 inches) is now ready and for sale by all the Booksellers and Stationers . . . Price $3.00. Our charges for mounting the same on plain frame and varnishing are . . . 50 cts. For framing in 2½ inch polished Black Walnut Frame, (also mounted and varnished) . . . $2.50.

Holzapfel & Eskuche, publishers
443 East Water Street.[6]

This particular view, printed in several colors, was quite handsome. Smaller views and those in two tones did not command as high a price. (Money was not the only exchange medium for views. Thaddeus Fowler reportedly accepted quantities of flour and beans on occasion for his town views.[7]) We may assume that the price of panoramic city plans increased during the 20th century, and therefore, the range in cost was probably from $1.00 to $5.00.

The most successful print publisher in the 19th century was the firm of Currier & Ives. Best remembered for their views of daily life in Victorian America, they also prepared bird's-eye views of New York City, Chicago, Boston, San Francisco, and Washington. However, they were not a leading panoramic map-making firm, and their distinctive views were primarily of large cities. Most post-Civil War panoramic maps were of decided parochial interest, highlighting small cities and towns, and were more detailed than the average Currier & Ives' city perspective.

Albert Ruger, Thaddeus Mortimer Fowler, Lucien R. Burleigh, Henry Wellge, and Oakley H. Bailey prepared more than 66 percent of the panoramic maps in the Library of Congress. Albert Ruger was the first to achieve success as a panoramic artist. The collections of the Library's Geography and Map Division contain 198 city maps drawn or published by Ruger or by Ruger & Stoner. The majority came from Ruger's personal collection, which the Library purchased in 1941 from John Ramsey of Canton, Ohio. Before this accession, there were only four Ruger city plans in the Geography and Map Division. Ruger, born in Prussia in 1829, emigrated to the United States and initially worked as a mason. While serving with the Ohio Volunteers during the Civil War, he drew views of Union campsites, among them Camp Chase in Ohio and Stephenson's Depot in Virginia. He continued to draw after the war, and his prints include a famous lithograph of Lincoln's funeral car passing the statehouse in Columbus, Ohio.[8]

By 1866 Ruger had settled in Battle Creek, Mich., where he began his prolific panoramic mapping career by sketching Michigan cities. Full descriptions of many Ruger views of Michigan cities are contained in John Cumming's *A Preliminary Checklist of 19th Century Lithographs of Michigan Cities and Towns*. Towns in some 20 states, ranging from New Hampshire to Minnesota and south to Georgia and Alabama, were sketched by Ruger. He continued his activity into the 1890's, moving his business to Chicago, Madison, Wis., and St. Louis as he sought new markets. Albert Ruger died in Akron, Ohio, on November 12, 1899. In the late 1860's Ruger formed a partnership with J. J. Stoner of Madison, Wis., and together they published numerous city panoramas. Ruger was particularly productive during the 1860's; in 1869 alone he produced more than 60 panoramic maps. In addition to city plans he drew views of university campuses, among them Notre Dame, Shurtleff College, and the University of Michigan.

The name which appears on the greatest number of panoramic maps in the collections of the Library of Congress is that of Thaddeus Mortimer Fowler. He was born in Lowell,

Mass., on December 21, 1842, and ran away from home at the age of 15. When the first call for military volunteers for the Civil War was issued by President Lincoln, Fowler was in Buffalo, N.Y. Although initially rejected because he was under age, after some maneuvering Fowler was sworn into the 21st Regiment of the New York Volunteers at Elmira, N.Y., in May 1861. He received an ankle wound at the Second Battle of Bull Run and was honorably discharged at Boston in February 1863, leaving the hospital on crutches after refusing amputation. He then visited army camps where he made tintypes of soldiers. In 1864 Fowler migrated to Madison, Wis., where he worked with his uncle J. M. Fowler, a photographer. He established his own panoramic map firm and in 1870 produced a view of Omro, Wis. This was followed the next year by panoramas of Peshtigo, Sheboygan Falls, and Waupaca, Wis.[9] The Boston Public Library has six views drawn and published by Fowler in the 1870's. During the intervening decade, he was employed as an artist by J. J. Stoner. Fowler moved from Madison around 1880 to northern New Jersey, first to the Oranges and later to Asbury Park. A panoramic map of Ocean Grove and Asbury Park which he published in 1881 is the earliest Fowler view in the Library of Congress collections.[10] Between 1881 and 1885, Fowler was located successively in Lewisburg and Shamokin, Pa., and in Trenton, N.J. On April 1, 1885, he moved with his family to Morrisville, Pa., where he maintained his headquarters for 25 years. One of the inconveniences of his profession was the recurring need to find new territory for his artistry. In a 1913 request for an increase in his military pension, Fowler noted that "although claiming home where my family was located—I was on the road as Publisher and Canvasser ever since the war."[11]

Morrisville served as a convenient operating center as Fowler began to draw and publish views of Pennsylvania, West Virginia, and Ohio cities. His production of Pennsylvania panoramas was greater than that of any other artist for a particular state. In the Library of Congress' collections are 134 separate Fowler views of Pennsylvania, representing 131 different towns. There are, moreover, an additional 53 Fowler views of Pennsylvania towns in the Pennsylvania State Archives

Thaddeus M. Fowler

and at Pennsylvania State University. This is an outstanding production record.

At various periods during his career, Fowler was associated with other panoramic artists. The association with James B. Moyer, of Myerstown, Pa., from 1889 to 1902 was particularly extensive and productive. Some city maps were also published under the imprints Fowler & Kelly, Fowler & Albert E. Downs, and Fowler & Browning. After 1910 Fowler prepared panoramic maps of cities in Connecticut, Massachusetts, New Jersey, and New York for Oakley H. Bailey, who marketed his prints as aero views.[12]

Throughout his career, which extended over 54 years, Thaddeus Fowler never ceased to find pleasure in drawing and publishing panoramic maps. In a letter written to his granddaughter in 1920, he expressed "an unadulterated joy"[13] while sketching a view of Middletown, N.Y. This was the expression of a man who at that time had been working at his profession 50 years! In the same letter Fowler alluded to some of the problems viewmakers encountered. He was in Allentown, Pa., in 1918, he recalled, preparing an aero view of the city, probably in association with Oakley H. Bailey. Airplanes and a dirigible circling the city were included in the trademark of the aero view to give the impression that some of the information was derived from aerial reconnaisance, which, of course, was not true. Some Allentown citizens noticed the view with the planes on the manuscript map. In the excitement engendered by World War I, Fowler was accused of being a German spy and was jailed. Members of his immediate family drove from Morrisville to identify their father, who suffered injury only to his pride in the incident. In the 1920 letter previously cited, Fowler also noted that Oakely H. Bailey had

taken up my job at Allentown where I left off. The Sec'y of the Chamber of Commerce was very much taken with the drawing as far as I had it done and promised to help. Mayor Gross was very gracious and also favored the idea very much. Quite a different reception Bailey had to mine. There's no doubt we will do well there.[14]

The Allentown panorama, the largest extant Fowler view, apparently was never published. The original drawing was presented to the Library in 1970 by Mrs. T. B. Fowler. The

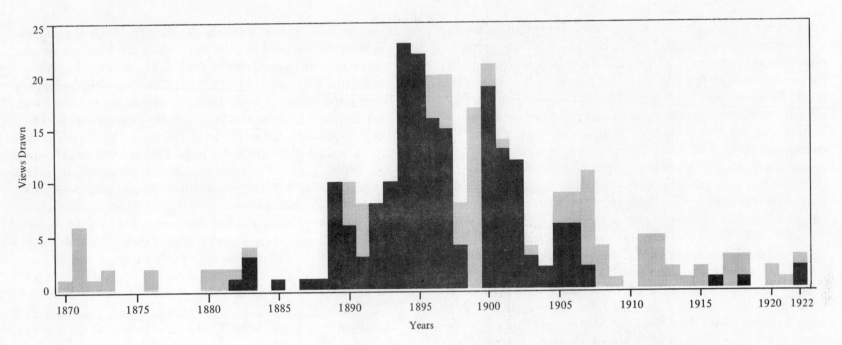

Views drawn by Thaddeus M. Fowler. Black represents views of Pennsylvania; gray represents views of other states.

magnificent pen-and-ink manuscript with grey wash, which measures 28 by 71 inches, engaged Thaddeus Fowler and Oakley Bailey for over four years. A feeling of the city's vitality was expressed by drawings of operating industrial plants, trains in motion, city thoroughfares filled with automobiles and pedestrians, and a group of fans watching a baseball game. The Allentown map was one of the last to which Fowler contributed. He died in March 1922 in his 80th year, following a fall on icy streets incurred while preparing a panorama of Port Jervis, N.Y. Fowler's career spanned the entire period of panoramic map production, and only Oakley H. Bailey shares this distinction.

The views of Thaddeus Fowler include cities and towns in at least 18 states and Canada.[15] To date, 301 separate Fowler panoramas have been identified. Of the 224 in the Library of Congress, the majority were acquired on copyright deposit. In 1943, 60 Fowler views of Pennsylvania and West Virginia were purchased from the Laurel Book Service, Hazleton, Pa., among which are 11 of the Library's 28 Fowler views of West Virginia.

In 1970 and 1971 the artist's daughter-in-law Mrs. T. B. (Roxana) Fowler and her family presented to the Library a collection of over 100 of his maps, 46 of them not previously in the Library's collections.

An analysis of Fowler views of Pennsylvania towns suggests that the panoramic artist concentrated on a specific geographical area in a given year, very likely to minimize transportation problems. From 1889 to 1894, for example, he sketched cities in eastern Pennsylvania. In 1889 he focused on Schuylkill County, from 1890 to 1892 he worked in the Scranton and Wilkes-Barre area, and the area north of Philadelphia was mapped in 1893. Views of cities between Morrisville and Chambersburg were made in 1894, and from 1895 to 1897 he worked in the western part of the state, especially around Pittsburgh, and in the northwest sector of Pennsylvania. In 1898 and 1899 Fowler sketched West Virginia towns and from 1900 to 1903 was back in western Pennsylvania. Subsequently he made trips to Maryland, Virginia, North Carolina, and Georgia to draw city plans and to investigate the possibility of expanding his trade into the South, which proved unsuccessful.

Fowler gained commissions for city plans by interesting citizens and civic groups in the idea of a panoramic map of their community. After one town had agreed to having a map made, he would seek to involve neighboring communities. By noting that he had already secured an agreement for a view from one town in the area, he would play on the pride, community spirit, and sense of competition of adjacent communities. By such promotional procedures he garnered commitments for panoramic maps from a limited geographical area, thus eliminating travel expenses. Similar methods were employed by Ruger, Stoner, and Burleigh.

Oakley H. Bailey, another outstanding panoramic map artist and publisher and a close friend of Thaddeus Fowler, was born of Quaker parents June 14, 1843, in Mahoning County, Ohio. He enrolled in Mount Union College, Alliance, Ohio, in 1862. His studies were disrupted temporarily in 1864, while he served with the 143d Ohio Volunteer Militia, Company F, but he returned to school after his service obligation and graduated from Mount Union in 1866. He taught briefly in the area school system, but in 1866 he left Ohio and entered business with his brother H. H. Bailey and edited a business directory of Ohio. His territory reached as far as Chicago, Ill., Indianapolis, and Minneapolis. In 1871 he turned to the profession of making panoramic maps. Bailey's career began in Madison, Wis., but by 1874 he had moved to Boston. From headquarters there and in New York City, Bailey published panoramic maps of American cities until the late 1920's, first under the name bird's-eye views and later as aero views.[16] His brother H. H. Bailey, who also drew views, was Oakley's partner for many years.

There are 68 Bailey items in the Library of Congress, and the Boston Public Library has more than 200 views drawn or published by Bailey between 1874 and 1891. A Bailey drawing of Atlantic City, measuring over seven feet in length, shows five or six miles of the famous boardwalk, myriad hotels, other buildings, and the ocean front. His maps were issued under the imprints of Oakley H. Bailey, Oakley H. Bailey & Co., O. H. Bailey & J. C. Hazen, Bailey & Fowler, Bailey & Hughes,

Bailey & Moyer, Fowler & Bailey, and Hughes & Bailey. In the 1920's the firm of Hughes & Cinquin produced panoramic maps under the sponsorship of Oakley H. Bailey, who had retired in 1927. Perhaps by that time Bailey's eyesight had become too weak to permit him to continue the tedious, close work required of a panoramic artist. He died on August 13, 1947, in Alliance, Ohio, at the age of 104.

When asked in 1932 why he had gone into the panoramic map business instead of farming, Bailey replied that at an early age he had realized that pastoral pursuits were filled with too many uncertainties. He chose instead the career of panoramic map publishing and remained active in it for 55 years, drawing and publishing maps of cities in some 20 northern states and Canada.[17] In a 1932 interview he further noted:

The business has been practically without competition as so few could give it the patience, care and skill essential to success. But now the airplane cameras are covering the territory and can put more towns on paper in a day than was possible in months by hand work formerly.[18]

Equally as prolific as Bailey in publishing maps of Northeastern U.S. cities was Lucien R. Burleigh of Troy, N.Y. During the 1880's Burleigh views of New York and New England were particularly popular. The Library of Congress has 136 Burleigh panoramic city plans. State and local archives in New York may contain even more of Burleigh's views. An 1883 Troy city directory listed Burleigh as a civil engineer. By 1886 he had become a lithographer and view publisher, publishing under the name Burleigh Lithographing Company. An advertisement in the 1886 city directory stated that the firm did fine work in all branches of engraving and printing, with "views of buildings and villages a specialty."[19] Burleigh published panoramic maps as late as 1892, but his most productive years were from 1885 to 1890. Views were published under his personal name and under the imprint Burleigh Lithographing Company or Burleigh Lithographing Establishment.

Henry Wellge, like Albert Ruger, was a midwestern panoramic map artist and publisher. He worked initially for J. J. Stoner but in the 1880's established his own company.

His views of towns in 24 states were issued under several imprints—Henry Wellge & Co., Norris, Wellge & Co., and the American Publishing Co. Among other noteworthy panoramic map artists were Herman Brosius, Rene Cinquin, Albert E. Downs, Eli S. Glover, Augustus Koch, George E. Norris, and George H. Walker. Walker was also a successful publisher of atlases and maps.

The urban areas in the Midwest and Eastern United States were of primary interest to panoramic map artists. Several of the artists began their careers in the Midwest, particularly in Madison, Wis., and during the 1860's and 1870's a large number of panoramic maps of Midwestern cities and towns appeared. By the late 1870's the Madison group had dispersed. Ruger and Stoner remained in that city, but Bailey and Fowler moved eastward to virgin territory. The latter two and Lucien Burleigh made the Middle Atlantic and New England states the chief production center for bird's-eye views during the 1880's and 1890's. It was in these areas, moreover, that the panoramic map business had its final flurry of activity in the 1920's.

During the 1860's and 1870's the major publishers and lithographers of panoramic maps were concentrated in the Chicago-Milwaukee area because of the proximity to the artists' center of Madison. Beck & Pauli Lithographers (Milwaukee), Joseph J. Stoner (Madison), and Merchants Lithographers and Chicago Lithographers (Chicago) were responsible for a large percentage of the panoramas. Adam Beck and Clemens J. Pauli operated one of the most active lithographic firms in this area, producing views drawn in 26 states. Beck and Pauli printed views from 1878 to 1889, being most active during the mid-1880's. Clemens J. Pauli tried his own hand at drawing and printing views in 1889.

Another active producer was Charles Shober, whose panoramas appeared under several imprints, including Charles Shober & Co., Shober & Carqueville Lithographing Co., and the Chicago Lithographing Co. Joseph J. Stoner was the Madison publisher most identified with the Milwaukee-Chicago area panoramic map business. Every major view artist except Lucien R. Burleigh had works published at one time or another by Stoner. By the 1880's publishers and lithographers on the east coast of the United States rivaled the Midwestern companies.

In the Far West[20] and the South panoramic maps never attained the popularity they achieved in the area north of the Mason-Dixon line, between Maine and Minnesota. Attempts to extend the industry to the South and the West were not particularly successful, although panoramic maps of a few cities in Alabama, Arkansas, Montana, New Mexico, North Dakota, South Dakota, and Colorado were produced. Views of communities in the state of Washington were drawn by Eli S. Glover and Henry Wellge in a span of one or two years in the 1870's or 1880's. Wellge's views of the state, for example, were all drawn in 1884. The South was economically unable to support views of their cities during Reconstruction, and northern canvassers probably would not have been welcome. More significantly, perhaps, the focal point of life in the South was the farm or plantation, not the village or town as in the Midwest and the Northeastern states.

Similarly, the panoramic map business never gained in popularity in Canada. The Library's collections contain only 12 panoramic maps of Canadian cities. The Public Archives of Canada has only 42 panoramic maps, of which three represent various editions of Fowler's view of Winnipeg, Manitoba.

The Library's collection includes the largest panoramic map published—Camille N. Dry's 1875 *Pictorial St. Louis; The Great Metropolis of the Mississippi Valley*, which was dedicated to the famous Mississippi River bridgebuilder Capt. James B. Eads. It was produced on 110 plates, which when trimmed and assembled created a panorama of the city measuring about 9 by 24 feet. Dry issued the panoramic map in an atlas, the preface of which included the following notes regarding its preparation:

A careful perspective, which required a surface of three hundred square feet, was then erected from a correct survey of the city, extending northward from Arsenal Island to the Water Works, a distance of about ten miles, on the river front; and from the Insane Asylum on he southwest to the Cemeteries on the northwest. Every foot of the vast territory within these limits has been carefully examined and topographically drawn

Plate 21.

One of the 110 plates from Camille N. Dry's Pictorial St. Louis; the Great Metropolis of the Mississippi Valley, *published in 1875.*

in perspective . . . and the faithfulness and accuracy with which this work has been done an examination of the pages will attest.

The St. Louis panorama evidently was prepared to show the city's progress at the United States Centennial celebration of 1876. The verso of each plate contains information on various aspects of St. Louis economic life, including businesses, professions, schools, churches, and governmental organizations. Every building in the area was drawn on the map, and 1,999 specific sites were identified by name. A note in the preface requests that any mistakes detected be looked upon with a lenient eye by an indulgent public "in view of the magnitude of the work, the originality of the idea, and the difficulties encountered in carrying it out." Dry's map of St. Louis is a magnificent extension of the normal single-sheet lithographic view and one of the crowning achievements of the art. Also impressive for their size and detail are the colored view of Washington (1883–84), which measures 4 by 5½ feet, and that of Baltimore (1869), measuring 5 × 11 feet, both published by the Sachses of Baltimore.

Although the separate print was the most common panoramic map format, views of cities and towns also appeared as illustrations in 19th-century state and county atlases. Credit was often not given to the artist in such publications, but some of the leading panoramic map artists probably prepared views for these atlases. Ruger, for example, prepared a landscape view for the title page of E. L. Hayes' 1877 atlas of the upper Ohio River and Valley. The town views in Andreas' 1875 Iowa atlas, although unsigned, also resemble Ruger's work.[21]

Surviving panoramic maps are very popular today and command premium prices from map and print dealers. Facsimile reproductions of panoramic maps are likewise in demand. Historic Urban Plans of Ithaca, N.Y., has published more than 50 facsimiles of low and high oblique angle views of American cities.

Panoramic maps give a pictorial record of Anglo-America's cities during the post-Civil War period and for many localities provide the sole 19th-century map. No other graphic form of this era so effectively captured the vitality of America's urban centers.

Notes

[1] "A 'Young' Old Timer," *Sebring (Ohio) Times*, 1932. The article is an interview with panoramic map artist Oakley H. Bailey. Our copy of the article is from Mrs. T. B. Fowler, Morrisville, Pa.

[2] The information on the Fowler view is derived from an interview with his daughter-in-law, Mrs. T. B. (Roxana) Fowler of Aberdeen, Md., in November 1971.

[3] From Hughes & Bailey's 1920 view of Derby, Conn., drawn by Thaddeus M. Fowler.

[4] Letter from Harold Hugo, president, Meriden Gravure Company, Meriden, Conn., to John Hébert, Feb. 1, 1972.

[5] "A 'Young' Old Timer," *Sebring (Ohio) Times*, 1932.

[6] View on file in the Geography and Map Division, Library of Congress.

[7] From interview with Mrs. T. B. (Roxana) Fowler, November 1971.

[8] John Cumming, comp., *A Preliminary Checklist of 19th Century Lithographs of Michigan Cities and Towns* (Mount Pleasant, Michigan, Clarke Historical Library, Central Michigan University, c1969), p. iii.

[9] The four Fowler views of Wisconsin are in the collections of the State Historical Society of Wisconsin, Madison, Wis.

[10] The 1880 Fowler view of Fargo, N. Dak., included in the Library's list of panoramic maps predates the 1881 New Jersey view. However, it is a photographic copy of an original in the New York Public Library.

[11] From Thaddeus Fowler's military pension records, National Archives, Washington, D.C.

[12] Information on Fowler from his military pension record, National Archives, and from an unpublished account of his life by his son, Thaddeus B. Fowler. A copy of the son's recollections was given to the author by James Raymond Warren, Sr., of Wheaton, Md. From that same source we learned that Fowler married Elizabeth Anna Dann in 1875 in Madison, Wis. Five children came of this union.

[13] Fowler to Ruth Fowler, Apr. 11, 1920. Ruth Fowler is now Mrs. Clarence Sinclair, Morrisville, Pa.

[14] Ibid.

[15] To our knowledge, an 1881 view of Winnipeg, now in the Public Archives of Canada, is his only Canadian view.

[16] "A 'Young' Old Timer," *Sebring (Ohio) Times*, 1932.

[17] Ibid.

[18] Ibid.

[19] *Troy, New York, Directory . . . 1886.* (Sampson, Murdock & Co.), p. 558.

[20] George Henry Goddard drew low oblique angle views of California towns in the 1850's. However, few California town panoramic maps appeared in the post-Civil War period.

[21] See E. L. Hayes, *Illustrated Atlas of the Upper Ohio River and Valley from Pittsburgh, Pa. to Cincinnati, Ohio. From United States official and special surveys . . .* (Philadelphia, Titus, Simmons & Titus, 1877), and Alfred T. Andreas, *A. T. Andreas' Illustrated Historical Atlas of the State of Iowa* (Chicago, Andreas Atlas Co., 1875).

Birmingham, Ala., 1885, with insets of some of the city's industrial firms.
Drawn and published by Norris, Wellge & Co.

Checklist

Alabama

No.	City and Date	Artist	Publisher	Lithographer or Printer	Map Size (Inches)
1	Anniston 1887		Henry Wellge & Co., Milwaukee, Wisconsin	Beck & Pauli, Lith., Milwaukee, Wisconsin	18×24½
2	Anniston 1888	E. S. Glover	E. S. Glover	Shober & Carqueville Litho. Co., Chicago	21×31
3	Anniston 1903		C. N. Dry	Charles Hart, Lith., New York	23½×34
4	Birmingham 1885	H. Wellge	Norris, Wellge & Co., Milwaukee, Wisconsin	Beck & Pauli, Litho., Milwaukee, Wisconsin	23×33
5	Birmingham (Business Section) 1903	C. N. Dry	C. N. Dry		6½×9½
6	Gadsden 1887	H. Welge [sic]	Henry Wellge & Co., Milwaukee, Wisconsin	Beck & Pauli Litho. Co., Milwaukee, Wisconsin	20½×26
7	Huntsville 1871	[Albert Ruger]		Ehrgott & Krebs Lith., Cincinnati	22×24½
8	Montgomery 1887	H. Wellge	Henry Wellge & Co., Milwaukee, Wisconsin	Beck & Pauli Lith. Co., Milwaukee, Wisconsin	25×36½
9	Selma 1887	H. Wellge	Henry Wellge & Co., Milwaukee, Wisconsin	Beck & Pauli Lith. Co., Milwaukee, Wisconsin	21½×33½
10	Tuscaloosa 1887	H. Wellge	Henry Wellge & Co., Milwaukee, Wisconsin	Beck & Pauli Lith. Co., Milwaukee, Wisconsin	20×25½

Arizona

No.	City and Date	Artist	Publisher	Lithographer or Printer	Map Size (Inches)
11	Phoenix 1885	C. J. Dyer Phoenix	C. J. Dyer, Phoenix	W. Byrnes, Lith., San Francisco; Schmidt Label & Litho. Co., San Francisco	22×33

Gadsden, Ala., 1887. Drawn and published by Henry Wellge & Co., Milwaukee, Wis.

PERSPECTIVE MAP OF THE CITY

GADSDEN, ALA.

COUNTY SEAT OF ETOWAH COUNTY

1887

Arkansas

No.	City and Date	Artist	Publisher	Lithographer or Printer	Map Size (Inches)
12	Hot Springs 1888	H. Wellge	Henry Wellge & Co., Milwaukee, Wisconsin	Beck & Pauli Lith. Co., Milwaukee, Wisconsin	16½×26½
13	Little Rock 1871	A. Ruger	A. Ruger		23×34
14	Little Rock 1887		Henry Wellge & Co., Milwaukee, Wisconsin	Beck & Pauli Lith. Co., Milwaukee, Wisconsin	21½×30
15	Texarkana, Arkansas and Texas 1888		Henry Wellge & Co., Milwaukee, Wisconsin	Beck & Pauli Co., Milwaukee, Wisconsin	16×26½
16	Van Buren 1888	H. Wellge	Henry Wellge & Co., Milwaukee, Wisconsin	Beck & Pauli Lith. Co., Milwaukee, Wisconsin	17½×25

California

No.	City and Date	Artist	Publisher	Lithographer or Printer	Map Size (Inches)
17	Bakersfield 1901		N. J. Stone, San Francisco	Britton & Rey, San Francisco	28×37½
18	Berkeley 1909		Charles Green, Berkeley, California		12½×28½
19	Columbia 1852	E. H. Goddard	Reproduced in 1970 by Historic Urban Plans, Ithaca, New York	Pollard & Britton's Lith. S. F.	12½×18
20	Eureka 1902		A. C. Noe & G. R. Georgeson	Britton & Rey, San Francisco	26½×38
21	Healdsburg and Russian River Valley 1876	E. S. Glover	Jordan Bros.	A. L. Bancroft & Co., San Francisco	17½×23
22	Lakeport 1888	Stanley Inchbold		Britton & Rey, San Francisco	18½×25½
23	Los Angeles 1857	Kuchel & Dressel, S. F.	Kuchel & Dressel. Reproduced in 1969 by Historic Urban Plans, Ithaca, New York	Britton & Rey	12×17¾

No.	City and Date	Artist	Publisher	Lithographer or Printer	Map Size (Inches)
24	Los Angeles 1873	A[lfred] E. Mathews	A. L. Bancroft & Co. San Francisco, Cal. Reproduced in 1970 by Historic Urban Plans, Ithaca, New York	A. L. Bancroft & Co.	13×20
25	Los Angeles 1877 (with Brooklyn Hights)	E. S. Glover	Brooklyn Land & Building Co., Los Angeles	A. L. Bancroft & Co., San Francisco	13×23½
26	Los Angeles, Santa Monica & Wilmington 1877	E. S. Glover, Los Angeles, Cal.	E. S. Glover, Los Angeles, Cal.		21×33½
27	Los Angeles 1891	H. B. Elliott	Southern California Land Co.	Elliott Publishing Co.	31×44
28	Los Angeles 1894	B. W. Pierce	Semi-Tropic Homestead Co.	B. W. Pierce; L[os] A[ngeles] Lith.	31×44
29	Los Angeles 1909	Worthington Gates	Bird's Eye View Publishing Co., Los Angeles	Western Lith. Co., Los Angeles	22½×36
30	Oakland 1900	F. L.	F. & H. Soderberg	Mutual L. & Lith. Co., San Francisco	28×43
30A	Pasadena 1893	B. W. Pierce	Wood & Church, Los Angeles. Reproduced in 1972 by Historic Urban Plans, Ithaca, New York	B. W. Pierce	23×34½
31	Placerville 1888	R. H. & L. Roethe	*Weekly Observer*. Reproduced in 1969 by Historic Urban Plans, Ithaca, New York	W. W. Elliott, Lith., S. F.	20½×28
32	Sacramento [189?]	R. H.	W. W. Elliott		24×36
33	San Diego 1876	E. S. Glover	Schneider & Kueppers, San Diego	A. L. Bancroft & Co., San Francisco	19×27
34	San Francisco 1847		Reproduced in 1968 by Historic Urban Plans, Ithaca, New York	Bosqui Eng. & Print. Co.	19×20½

No.	City and Date	Artist	Publisher	Lithographer or Printer	Map Size (Inches)
35	San Francisco 1868	George H. Goddard	Snow & May	Britton & Rey, San Francisco	27½×41
35A	San Francisco 1868	W. Vallance Gray & C. B. Gifford	W. Vallance Gray & C. B. Gifford. Reproduced in 197– by The American West Publishing Co., Palo Alto, Calif.	W. Vallance Gray & C. B. Gifford	14½×20½
36	San Francisco 1875	Frederick Marriott, L. R. Townsend, E. Wyneken & J. Mendenhall		Britton & Rey, San Francisco	20½×31
37	San Francisco & Surrounding Country 1876	G. H. Goddard	Snow & May	Britton & Rey, San Francisco	33×47
38	San Francisco 1878	C. R. Parsons	Currier & Ives, New York. Reproduced in 1968 by Historic Urban Plans, Ithaca, New York		21×27½
39	San Gabriel [1893]		D. D. Morse		14×20½
40	San José 1869	W. Vallance Gray & C. B. Gifford	Geo. H. Hare, San José	W. Vallance Gray & C. B. Gifford	19½×28
41	San José 1875	C. B. Gifford	W. C. Gifford, San José	A. L. Bancroft & Co., San Francisco	19×27
42	San José 1901	F. L.	N. J. Stone Company, San Francisco, Cal.	Britton & Rey, S. F.	28½×42
43	San Mateo 1931		Aug. Chevalier		12½×24
44	San Mateo Park 1905		Baldwin & Howell		9×7½
45	Santa Barbara 1877	E. S. Glover	E. S. Glover	A. L. Bancroft & Co., San Francisco	20½×30½
46	Santa Barbara 1896				5½×7½

No.	City and Date	Artist	Publisher	Lithographer or Printer	Map Size (Inches)
47	Santa Barbara 1898		P. E. Gifford	Los Angeles Litho. Co.	25×36½
48	Santa Rosa 1876	E. S. Glover	Wm. M. Evans	A. L. Bancroft & Co., San Francisco	17½×25½
49	Sonora 1852		G. H. Goddard	Pollard & Brittons, S. F.	Photostatic negative, 11×13. (Wagner Collection)
50	Stockton 1895		Dakin Publishing Co.		22×33
51	Stockton 1895		Dakin Publishing Co., San Francisco		27½×40
52	Stockton 1895		Dakin Publishing Co., San Francisco; John H. Mitchell		27×37½
53	Stockton 1895		Dakin Publishing, San Francisco		27×40

Colorado

No.	City and Date	Artist	Publisher	Lithographer or Printer	Map Size (Inches)
54	Black Hawk 1882		J. J. Stoner, Madison, Wisconsin	Beck & Pauli, Lith., Milwaukee, Wisconsin	8×19
55	Buena Vista 1882		J. J. Stoner, Madison, Wisconsin	Beck & Pauli, Lith., Milwaukee, Wisconsin	10×14
56	Canon City 1882	H. Wellge	J. J. Stoner, Madison, Wisconsin	Beck & Pauli, Lith., Milwaukee, Wisconsin	10×16½
56A	Central City & Blackhawk 1873	E. S. Glover	Reproduced in 1971 by Historic Urban Plans, Ithaca, New York	Strobridge & Co., Lith., Cincinnati, O.	15½×17¼
57	Central City 1887		John Kohfahl, New York	Robert A. Welcke, New York	16×19½
58	Colorado Springs, Colorado City & Manitou 1882		J. J. Stoner, Madison, Wisconsin	Beck & Pauli, Lith., Milwaukee, Wisconsin	15×23

No.	City and Date	Artist	Publisher	Lithographer or Printer	Map Size (Inches)
58A	Colorado Springs 1890		American Publishing Co., Milwaukee, Wis.		18×42
59	Colorado Springs 1909		Benford-Bryan Publishing Co., Denver		13×18½
60	Cripple Creek & Victor 1896		Phillips & DesJardins	The Western Litho. Co., Denver	28×37
61	Denver 1874		Reproduced in 1970 by Historic Urban Plans, Ithaca, New York	[Strobridge & Co., Cincinnati, Ohio]	18×28
62	Denver 1874		Reproduced [in 1971] from an original lithograph in the State Historical Society of Colorado	Strobridge & Co., Cincinnati, Ohio	14½×23
63	Denver 1881	J. H. Flett			Photographic copy, 9×14
64	Denver 1887		Rocky Mountain News Printing Co., Denver, Colorado	Mills Eng. Co., Denver	19×24
65	Denver 1889	H. Wellge	American Publishing Co., Milwaukee, Wisconsin		27½×42½
65A	Denver (Harlem & Jacksons Broadway Heights Devel.) 1907	A. E. Mitchell	A. F. Haraszthy & W. J. Voit, Colorado Land Headquarters, Denver, Colo.	Denver Engraving Co.	19½×25
66	Denver 1908		Bird's Eye View Publishing Co., Denver	The Denver Lith. Co., Denver	42½×62
67	Fort Collins 1899	M. Houghton			7×13
67A	Georgetown 1874	E. S. Glover	Reproduced in 1971 by Historic Urban Plans, Ithaca, New York	Strobridge & Co., Lith., Cincinnati, O.	16×17

No.	City and Date	Artist	Publisher	Lithographer or Printer	Map Size (Inches)
68	Golden 1882		J. J. Stoner, Madison, Wisconsin	Beck & Pauli, Lith., Milwaukee, Wisconsin	11×23½
69	Greeley 1882		J. J. Stoner, Madison, Wisconsin	Beck & Pauli, Lith., Milwaukee, Wisconsin	15×23
70	Gunnison 1882		J. J. Stoner, Madison, Wisconsin	Beck & Pauli, Lith., Milwaukee, Wisconsin	11×21
71	Leadville 1879	Augustus Koch	Augustus Koch	Ramsey, Millett & Hudson, Kansas City, Missouri	23×33½
72	Leadville 1882	H. Wellge	J. J. Stoner, Madison, Wisconsin	Beck & Pauli, Lith., Milwaukee, Wisconsin	19×26½
73	Maysville 1882		J. J. Stoner, Madison, Wisconsin	Beck & Pauli, Lith., Milwaukee, Wisconsin	7×15
74	Pueblo 1890		American Publishing Co., Milwaukee, Wisconsin		36×26
75	Salida 1882		J. J. Stoner, Madison, Wisconsin	Beck & Pauli, Lith., Milwaukee, Wisconsin	10×16½
76	Trinidad 1882		J. J. Stoner, Madison, Wisconsin	Beck & Pauli, Lith., Milwaukee, Wisconsin	13×17½

Connecticut

No.	City and Date	Artist	Publisher	Lithographer or Printer	Map Size (Inches)
77	Ansonia 1921		Hughes & Bailey, Waterbury, Connecticut	[Meriden Gravure Co., Meriden, Conn.]	22½×32½
78	Bristol 1889	Geo. E. Norris, Brockton, Mass.	Geo. E. Norris, Brockton, Mass.	The Burleigh Lith. Est., Troy, New York	19½×31½
79	Bristol 1907		Hughes & Bailey, New York		31×35
80	Derby 1920	[T. M. Fowler]	Hughes & Bailey, New York		8×10 film negative
81	Jewett City 1889		L. R. Burleigh, Troy, New York	The Burleigh Lith. Est., Troy, New York	16×26½

No.	City and Date	Artist	Publisher	Lithographer or Printer	Map Size (Inches)
82	Manchester 1914		Hughes & Bailey, New York	[Franklin Engraving Co., Boston, Mass.]	27×36½
83	Meriden 1918	T. M. Fowler (T. M. Fowler Map Coll. 65)	Hughes & Bailey, New York & Boston	[Meriden Gravure Co., Meriden, Conn.]	25×35½
84	Middletown 1877		O. H. Bailey & Co.		25×29
85	Middletown 1915	T. M. Fowler (T. M. Fowler Map Coll. 80)	Hughes & Bailey, New York	[Meriden Gravure Co., Meriden, Conn. & National Process Co., N.Y.]	25×35½
86	Naugatuck 1906		Hughes & Bailey, New York		27×34
87	New Haven 1879	O. H. Bailey & J. C. Hazen, Boston	O. H. Bailey & J. C. Hazen, Boston		29½×38
88	New London 1911		Hughes & Bailey, New York		32×39½
89	New Milford 1906		Hughes & Bailey, New York		27×30
90	Norwalk, South Norwalk and East Norwalk 1899		Landis & Hughes, New York		32½×44½
91	Norwich 1876	O. H. Bailey & Co.	O. H. Bailey & Co.	C. H. Vogt, Lith., Milwaukee, Wisconsin; J. Knauber & Co.	22½×34½
92	Norwich 1912		Hughes & Bailey, New York	[Hughes & Bailey, New York]	33×39½
93	Plainville 1878	O. H. Bailey & J. C. Hazen, Boston	O. H. Bailey & J. C. Hazen, Boston	C. H. Vogt	19×24½
94	Plainville 1907		Hughes & Bailey, New York		19×29
95	Shelton 1919		Hughes & Bailey, Boston	[Meriden Gravure Co., Meriden, Conn.]	20×31

No.	City and Date	Artist	Publisher	Lithographer or Printer	Map Size (Inches)
96	Southington 1914		Hughes & Bailey	[Consolidated Engraving Co. & Federal Engraving Co., Boston, Mass.]	28×36
97	South Manchester 1880	(T. M. Fowler Map Coll. 1)	O. H. Bailey & Co., Boston		18½×24½
98	Torrington 1907		Hughes & Bailey, New York		29×36
99	Wallingford 1905 (with inset of city in 1852)		Hughes & Bailey, New York		26×34
100	Waterbury 1899		Landis & Hughes, New York		36×44
101	Waterbury 1917	T. M. Fowler (T. M. Fowler Map Coll. 2)	Hughes & Bailey, Boston	[Meriden Gravure Co., Meriden, Conn.; Tudor Press, Boston]	23×32
102	Watertown 1918		Hughes & Bailey, Boston	[Meriden Gravure Co., Meriden, Conn.]	22½×34½
103	Willimantic 1909		Bailey & Hughes, New York		29×33
104	Winsted 1908		O. H. Bailey, New York		32×34

Delaware

No.	City and Date	Artist	Publisher	Lithographer or Printer	Map Size (Inches)
105	Clayton 1885				Photostatic negative copy, 16½×18
106	Wilmington 1874 (with inset of the city in 1770)	H. H. Bailey & Co.	H. H. Bailey & Co.	G. W. Lewis, Lith., Albany, New York	20×39

District of Columbia

No.	City and Date	Artist	Publisher	Lithographer or Printer	Map Size (Inches)
107	Washington 1872	Geo. A. Morrison	W. H. & O. H. Morrison		14½×20

No.	City and Date	Artist	Publisher	Lithographer or Printer	Map Size (Inches)
108	Washington 1882	Theo. R. Davis (from photographs by W. H. Jackson)	Reproduced in 1965 by Historic Urban Plans, Ithaca, New York		16×20
109	Washington 1883–84	Adolph Sachse	A. Sachse & Co., Baltimore, Maryland	A. Sachse & Co., Baltimore, Maryland	48×65
110	Washington 1883 (Part Showing Georgetown, Foggy Bottom and Potomac Waterfront)		A. Sachse & Co., Baltimore, Maryland		41×33
111	Washington 1892		Currier & Ives, New York. Reproduced in 1970 by Historic Urban Plans, Ithaca, New York		19×27½

Florida

No.	City and Date	Artist	Publisher	Lithographer or Printer	Map Size (Inches)
112	Green Cove Springs, 1885		Norris, Wellge & Co., Milwaukee, Wisconsin	Beck & Pauli, Litho., Milwaukee, Wisconsin	19½×27
113	Jacksonville 1876	Augustus Koch	Alvord, Kellog & Campbell		25×30½
114	Jacksonville 1893	Augustus Koch	Augustus Koch; Hudson-Kimberly Pub. Co., Kansas City, Missouri		28½×39
115	Lake City 1885	H. Wellge	Norris, Wellge & Co., Milwaukee, Wisconsin	Beck & Pauli, Litho., Milwaukee, Wisconsin	15×23
116	Longwood 1885	G. A. Miller	P. A. Demens & Co.	Forbes Co. Photo Lith.	22×34
117	Pensacola 1885	H. Wellge	Norris, Wellge & Co., Milwaukee, Wisconsin	Beck & Pauli, Lith., Milwaukee, Wisconsin	21×26½
118	Tallahassee 1885	H. Wellge	Norris, Wellge & Co., Milwaukee, Wisconsin	Beck & Pauli, Litho., Milwaukee, Wisconsin	17×23½

No.	City and Date	Artist	Publisher	Lithographer or Printer	Map Size (Inches)
119	Tallahassee 1926		James Wynne		19×15

Georgia

120	Albany 1885		Norris, Wellge & Co., Milwaukee, Wisconsin	Beck & Pauli, Litho., Milwaukee, Wisconsin	14½×23½
121	Altanta 1871	A. Ruger, St. Louis, Mo.	A. Ruger, St. Louis, Mo.		20½×27¾
122	Atlanta 1892	Aug. Koch	H. G. Saunders & W. L. Kline	Hughes Litho. Co., Chicago	33½×52
123	Atlanta 1919		Foote & Davies Co.		18×30
124	Columbus 1886	H. Wellge	Henry Wellge & Co., Milwaukee, Wisconsin	Beck & Pauli Lith. Co., Milwaukee, Wisconsin	24½×36
125	Cordele 1908	A. E. Downs, Boston, Mass. (T. M. Fowler Map Coll. 3)	T. M. Fowler & A. E. Downs, Morrisville, Pa.		18½×29
126	Fitzgerald 1908	T. M. Fowler, Morrisville, Pa.	T. M. Fowler, Morrisville, Pa.		23×29
127	Macon 1887	H. Wellge	Henry Wellge & Co., Milwaukee, Wisconsin	Beck & Pauli Lith. Co., Milwaukee, Wisconsin	23×34½
128	Macon 1912		J. W. Burke Co.		14×24½
129	Ocilla 1908	T. M. Fowler, Morrisville, Pa.	T. M. Fowler, Morrisville, Pa.		19×23
130	Quitman 1885		Norris, Wellge & Co., Milwaukee, Wisconsin	Beck & Pauli, Litho., Milwaukee, Wisconsin	12×16½
131	Tallapoosa 1892	Geo. E. Norris, Brockton, Mass.	Geo. E. Norris, Brockton, Mass.	The Burleigh Litho. Co., Troy, New York	25×31½
132	Thomasville 1885	H. Wellge	Norris Wellge & Co., Milwaukee, Wisconsin	Beck & Pauli, Lith., Milwaukee, Wisconsin	18×25½
133	Thomasville 1896	Henry Moller			5½×9

No.	City and Date	Artist	Publisher	Lithographer or Printer	Map Size (Inches)

Idaho

134	Hailey & Wood River Valley 1884	A. E. Browning, Salt Lake City	A. E. Browning	The Collier & Cleveland Lith. Co., Denver, Colorado	19×23½

Illinois

No.	City and Date	Artist	Publisher	Lithographer or Printer	Map Size (Inches)
135	Alton 1867	A. Ruger		Chicago Lithographing Co.	20⅛×28½
136	Aurora 1867	A. Ruger		Chicago Lithographing Co., Chicago	20½×27¾
137	Aurora 1882	H. Brosius	J. J. Stoner, Madison, Wisconsin	Beck & Pauli, Lith., Milwaukee, Wisconsin	20½×32
138	Batavia 1869	A. Ruger		Merchants' Lithographing Co., Chicago	17¾×22
139	Belleville 1867	A. Ruger		Chicago Lithographing Co.	19¾×27½
140	Bloomington 1867	A. Ruger		Chicago Lithographing Co.	19¾×28
141	Cairo 1867	A. Ruger		Chicago Lithographing Co.	19¾×28¼
142	Cairo 1888	H. Wellge	Henry Wellge & Co., Milwaukee, Wisconsin	Beck & Pauli Lith. Co., Milwaukee, Wisconsin	22×33½
143	Centralia 1867	A. Ruger		Chicago Lithographing Co.	19½×28
144	Champaign 1869	A. Ruger		Chicago Lithogr. Co., Chicago	20¼×26½
145	Chenoa 1869	[Albert Ruger]			8¾×14¼
146	Chicago 1857	Chr[istian] Inger; J. T. Palmatary	Braunhold & Sonne. Additions by Charles Sonne	Herline & Hensel, Phila.	In 2 parts each 47×41
147	Chicago [1860]				5×8
148	Chicago 1868 (Inset Chicago in 1820)	A. Ruger		Chicago Lithographing Co., Chicago	19¾×35

No.	City and Date	Artist	Publisher	Lithographer or Printer	Map Size (Inches)
149	Chicago 1871	Theodore R. Davis	*Harper's Weekly.* Reproduced in 1969 by Historic Urban Plans, Ithaca, New York		14¼×20½
150	Chicago 1892		Currier & Ives		23×33
151	Chicago 1892 (Inset Chicago 1832)		Peter Roy, Chicago		19×32½
152	Chicago 1893		Reynertson & Beckerman, Chicago	Eagle Lith. Co., Chicago	32½×46
153	Chicago (Business District) 1898		Poole Bros., Chicago		In 4 parts, each 21½×29
154	Chicago (Central Business Section) 1915		Arno B. Reincke		Photographic print, 10½×16
155	Chicago (Central Business Section) 1916		Arno B. Reincke, Chicago		20×30½
156	Clinton 1869	A. Ruger		Merchant's Lithographing Co., Chicago	17×22½
157	Danville 1869	A. Ruger		Chicago Lithogr. Co., Chicago	18¼×26
158	Decatur 1869	A. Ruger		Chicago Lithogr. Co.	20×25½
159	Elgin 1880	A. B. Upham	A. B. Upham	Shober & Carqueville Lith. Co., Chicago	19½×24½
160	El Paso 1869	A. Ruger		Chicago Lithographg. Co.	14×21
161	Geneva 1869	A. Ruger		Merchant's Lithographing Company, Chicago	18¾×22½
162	Highland 1894		J. S. Hoerner, Highland, Illinois	Heinicke-Fiegel Litho. Co., St. Louis	17×30½
163	Homer 1869	A. Ruger		Merchants Lithographing Company, Chicago	9½×12½
164	Kankakee 1869	A. Ruger	Ruger & Stoner, Madison, Wisconsin	Chicago Lithog. Co., Chicago	21×26

No.	City and Date	Artist	Publisher	Lithographer or Printer	Map Size (Inches)
165	Lincoln 1869	[Albert Ruger]	Ruger & Stoner	Merchant's Lithographing Co., Chicago, Ills.	20×26
166	Loda 1869	A. Ruger		Chicago Lith. Co.	13×19¾
167	Manteno 1869	A. Ruger		Merchant's Lithogr. Co., Chicago	9½×12½
167A	Mattoon 1884	J. W. Smith		Shober & Carqueville Lith. Co., Chicago	19½×29¼
168	Moline 1869	[Albert Ruger]	Ruger & Stoner, Madison, Wisconsin	Chicago Lithogr. Co.	17×21¾
169	Moline 1873	A. Hageboeck, Davenport, Iowa	A. Hageboeck, Davenport, Iowa	A. Hageboeck, Davenport, Iowa	9×26
170	Moline 1889	H. Wellge	American Publishing Co., Milwaukee, Wisconsin		19×27
171	Monmouth 1869	A. Ruger		Merchant's Lithographing Co., Chicago	20×26
172	Mount Sterling 1869	A. Ruger		Chicago Lithographing Co.	15½×22
173	Mount Vernon 1881	H. Brosius	S. C. Polk, Mount Vernon, Illinois; J. J. Stoner, Madison, Wisconsin	Beck & Pauli, Lith., Milwaukee, Wisconsin	14×24½
174	Naperville 1869	[Albert Ruger]	Ruger & Stoner, Madison, Wis.	Merchant's Lithographing Co., Chicago	18¼×23¼
175	Nauvoo [1855]	Herrmann J. Meyer, New York	Herrmann J. Meyer, New York		6×7
176	New Salem 1831–1837	Arthur L. Brown	R. J. Onstott, Mason City, Ill. (1909)	J. W. Franks & Sons, Peoria, Ill.	19×32
176A	Ottawa, 1895	Clemens J. Pauli, Milwaukee, Wis.	Clemens J. Pauli, Milwaukee, Wis.		8×10 film negative
177	Paxton 1869	A. Ruger		Merchants Lithographing Co., Chicago, Ills.	15×20
178	Peoria 1867	A. Ruger		Chicago Lithographing Co.	20×34
179	Pontiac 1869	A. Ruger		Merchant's Lithographing Company, Chicago	17×22

No.	City and Date	Artist	Publisher	Lithographer or Printer	Map Size (Inches)
180	Princeton 1870	Ruger & Stoner, Madison, Wisconsin		Chicago Lithogr. Co., Chicago	20×26
181	Rockford 1880		J. J. Stoner, Madison, Wisconsin	Beck & Pauli, Lith., Milwaukee, Wisconsin	18½×27½
182	Rockford 1891				26×41
183	Rock Island 1869	[Albert Ruger]	Ruger & Stoner, Madison, Wis.	Chicago Lithogr. Co., Chicago	19¾×25¾
184	Rock Island 1874	A. Hageboeck, Davenport, Iowa	A. Hageboeck, Davenport, Iowa	A. Hageboeck, Davenport, Iowa	8×25
185	Rock Island 1889	H. Wellge	American Publishing Co., Milwaukee, Wisconsin		27½×41
186	Sandwich 1869	A. Ruger		Chicago Lith. Co., Chicago	17½×22
187	Shelbyville 1869	A. Ruger		Merchant's Lithographing Co., Chicago, Ills.	19¾×25¾
188	Springfield 1867	A. Ruger		Chicago Lithographing Co.	20×33¾
189	Urbana 1869	A. Ruger		Chicago Lithogr. Co., Chicago	17½×22
190	Young America 1869	A. Ruger	Ruger & Stoner, Madison, Wisconsin	Chicago Lith. Co., Chicago	14×20

Indiana

No.	City and Date	Artist	Publisher	Lithographer or Printer	Map Size (Inches)
191	Attica 1869	A. Ruger		Chicago Lithogr. Co., Chicago	15½×21¾
191A	Cambridge City 1871	T. M. Fowler & H. H. Bailey	T. M. Fowler & H. H. Bailey	Milwaukee Lith. & Eng. Co.; C. H. Vogt, Lith.	Photostat, 17½×21½
192	Delphi 1868	A. Ruger		Merchants Lithographing Co., Chicago	18½×24¾
193	Evansville 1888	H. Wellge	American Publishing Co., Milwaukee, Wisconsin		27×40½

No.	City and Date	Artist	Publisher	Lithographer or Printer	Map Size (Inches)
194	Fort Wayne 1868 (Inset Fort Wayne 1825)	A. Ruger		Chicago Lithogr. Co.	21½×28
195	Fort Wayne 1907		B. J. Griswold	W. W. Hixson, Rockford, Illinois	In 2 parts, each 37×25
196	Kokomo 1868	A. Ruger		Merchants Lithographing Co., Chicago	20×25½
197	Lafayette 1868	A. Ruger		Chicago Lith. Co.	22×27½
198	Michigan City 1869	A. Ruger		Merchant's Lithographing Co., Chicago	20×28
199	Michigan City 1869	[Albert Ruger]		Merchants Lithographing Co., Chicago	17×27½
200	Peru 1868	[Albert Ruger]			20×25½
201	Richmond 1884	Albert Downs	O. H. Bailey & Co., Boston	J. W. C. Gilman & Co.	28×39½
202	South Bend 1866	A. Ruger, Battle Creek, Mich.	A. Ruger, Battle Creek, Mich.	Chicago Lithographing Co., Chicago	21×28½
203	South Bend 1874	[Albert Ruger]	J. J. Stoner, Madison, Wisconsin	Chas. Shober & Co., Chicago Lith. Co.	19½×26
204	South Bend 1890	C. J. Pauli Milwaukee, Wis.	C. J. Pauli, Milwaukee, Wis.		28×40
205	Terre Haute 1880			Beck & Pauli, Milwaukee, Wisconsin	24×40

Iowa

No.	City and Date	Artist	Publisher	Lithographer or Printer	Map Size (Inches)
206	Blairstown 1868	A. Ruger		Merchant's Lith. Co.	9¾×12¼
207	Burlington 1889	H. Wellge	American Publishing Co., Milwaukee, Wisconsin		22×32¼
208	Cedar Rapids 1868	A. Ruger		Chicago Lith. Co.	21½×26

No.	City and Date	Artist	Publisher	Lithographer or Printer	Map Size (Inches)
209	Council Bluffs 1868	A. Ruger		Merchant's Lith. Co., Chicago	22×27½
210	Davenport 1888	H. Wellge	American Publishing Co., Milwaukee, Wisconsin		24×40
211	Decorah 1870		Ruger & Stoner, Madison, Wisconsin	Merchant's Lith. Co., Chicago	19×22
212	Des Moines 1868	A. Ruger		Merchant's Lith. Co., Chicago	22×28½
213	De Witt 1868	[Albert Ruger]			20×26
214	Dubuque 1889	H. Wellge	American Publishing Co.		27×40
215	Fort Madison 1889	H. Wellge	American Publishing Co.		17×28
216	Gutenberg 1869		Ruger & Stoner, Madison, Wisconsin	Merchant's Lith. Co., Chicago	16½×21½
217	Iowa City 1868	A. Ruger		Chicago Lith. Co.	20¼×26
218	Lyons 1868	A. Ruger		Merchant's Lith. Co., Chicago	21½×28½
219	McGregor & North McGregor 1869		Ruger & Stoner, Madison, Wisconsin	Chicago Lith. Co.	21×22
220	Marengo 1868	A. Ruger		Merchant's Lith. Co.	22×26
221	Marion 1868	A. Ruger		Merchant's Lith. Co.	20½×26½
222	Marshalltown 1868	[Albert Ruger]			20×26
223	Montana 1868	A. Ruger		Chicago Lith. Co.	20×26
224	Newton 1868	A. Ruger		Merchant's Lith. Co., Chicago	21×26½
225	Sioux City 1889	Henry Wellge	H. Wellge & Co.	Beck & Pauli Lith. Co., Milwaukee, Wisconsin	25½×37

No.	City and Date	Artist	Publisher	Lithographer or Printer	Map Size (Inches)

Kansas

226	Atchison 1869	A. Ruger		Merchants Lithographing Co., Chicago	20½×25½
227	Girard [1879] (Inset in map of Crawford County by W. J. Eldridge [1879])				8×10 Photograph Negative
228	Herington 1887 [In L. H. Everts & Co., *The Official State Atlas of Kansas . . . 1887*, p. 260]				13×15
229	Lawrence 1869	[Albert Ruger]			20¾×26½
230	Leavenworth 1869	A. Ruger		Chicago Lithographing Co.	21¾×27¾
231	Topeka 1869	A. Ruger		Chicago Lithographing Co.	20×26
232	Wyandotte 1869 (now Kansas City)	C. Hafften; A. Ruger		Merchants Lith. Co., Chicago, Ill.	11½×18

Kentucky

233	Bowling Green 1871	A. Ruger		Chicago Litho. Co.	23×26
234	Frankfort 1871	[Albert Ruger]		Ehrgott & Krebs, Lith., Cincinnati, Ohio	23×24
235	Lexington 1871	[Albert Ruger]		Ehrgott & Krebs, Lith., Cincinnati, Ohio	23×28
236	Louisville 1876	A. Ruger		Chas. Shober & Co., Props., Chicago Lith. Co.	20×26
237	Louisville 1883	W. F. Clarke	M. P. Levyeau & Co., Cincinnati, Ohio & Louisville, Kentucky		23×34½

No.	City and Date	Artist	Publisher	Lithographer or Printer	Map Size (Inches)
238	Paducah 1889	J. Blanton		The Krebs Lith. Co., Cincinnati, Ohio	28×40
239	Paris 1870	[Albert Ruger]			22×25

Louisiana

No.	City and Date	Artist	Publisher	Lithographer or Printer	Map Size (Inches)
240	New Orleans 1851	Th. Muller	Reproduced in 1970 by Historic Urban Plans, Ithaca, New York	Th. Muller	15×20¾
241	New Orleans 1863	J. Wells; W. Ridgway	Virtue & Co.		7½×8
242	Shreveport 1872	H. Brosius			22½×28½

Maine

No.	City and Date	Artist	Publisher	Lithographer or Printer	Map Size (Inches)
243	Bar Harbor 1886		G. W. Morris, Portland, Maine	Geo. H. Walker & Co., Boston	20×25
244	Eastport 1879	J. J. Stoner, Madison, Wisconsin			Photostatic negative 15½×21½
245	Houlton 1894	Geo. E. Norris, Brockton, Mass.	Geo. E. Norris, Brockton, Mass.		18½×27
246	Livermore Falls 1889	Geo. E. Norris, Brockton, Mass.	Geo. E. Norris, Brockton, Mass.	Burleigh Lithographing Establishment, Troy, N.Y.	13×21½
246A	Monhegan 1896	Bert [Albert F.] Poole			17½×21¾
247	Peak's Island 1886	JC	G. W. Morris, Portland, Me.	Geo. H. Walker & Co., Boston	19½×32
248	Pittsfield 1889	Geo. E. Norris, Brockton, Mass.	Geo. E. Norris, Brockton, Mass.	The Burleigh Lith. Est., Troy, New York	16×22½
249	Portland 1876	Jos. Warner	J. J. Stoner, Madison, Wis.	Chas. Shober & Co., Chicago Litho'g Co.	23×35

No.	City and Date	Artist	Publisher	Lithographer or Printer	Map Size (Inches)
250	Presque Isle 1894		Geo. E. Norris, Brockton, Mass.		16×23½
251	Sanford 1889	Geo. E. Norris, Brockton, Mass.	Geo. E. Norris, Brockton, Mass.	The Burleigh Lith. Est., Troy, New York	15×26

Maryland

No.	City and Date	Artist	Publisher	Lithographer or Printer	Map Size (Inches)
252	Annapolis 1864		Chas. Magnus, New York. Reproduced in 1967 by Historic Urban Plans, Ithaca, New York		14×17
253	Baltimore 1850	E. Sachse	Casimir Bohn. Reproduced in 1967 by Historic Urban Plans, Ithaca, New York	E. Sachse & Co., Baltimore, Maryland	21×28
254	Baltimore 1869		E. Sachse & Co., Baltimore, Maryland	E. Sachse & Co., Baltimore, Maryland	In 4 parts: 62×34, 62×31, 62×32, 62×34
255	Baltimore 1911	Edward W. Spofford	Norman T. A. Munder & Co., Baltimore, Maryland	Norman T. A. Munder & Co., Baltimore, Maryland	20×30½
256	Chestertown 1907	T. M. Fowler (T. M. Fowler Map Coll. 79)	Fowler & Kelley, Morrisville, Pennsylvania		21×25½
257	Cumberland 1906	Thaddeus M. Fowler, Morrisville, Pennsylvania	Fowler & Kelly, Morrisville, Pennsylvania		15×20
258	Elkton 1907	[T. M. Fowler] (T. M. Fowler Map Coll. 59)	Fowler & Kelly, Morrisville, Pennsylvania		18×22
259	Frostburg 1905	T. M. Fowler, Morrisville, Pa. (T. M. Fowler Map Coll. 4)	T. M. Fowler, Morrisville, Pa.		20½×25
260	Havre de Grace 1907	T. M. Fowler, Morrisville, Pa.	Fowler & Kelly, Morrisville, Pa.		20½×23

No.	City and Date	Artist	Publisher	Lithographer or Printer	Map Size (Inches)
261	Mountain Lake Park 1906		Fowler & Kelly, Morrisville, Pennsylvania		22½×29½
262	Oakland 1906	Fowler & Kelly, Morrisville, Pa.	Fowler & Kelly, Morrisville, Pa.		16×20½
263	Rising Sun 1907	T. M. Fowler, Morrisville, Pa.	Fowler & Kelly, Morrisville, Pa.		17½×20½

Massachusetts

No.	City and Date	Artist	Publisher	Lithographer or Printer	Map Size (Inches)
263A	Amesbury & Salisbury Mills 1880		E. H. Bigelow, Framingham, Mass.	Beck & Pauli, Milwaukee, Wis.	8×10 photograph
264	Amesbury 1890	Geo. E. Norris, Brockton, Mass.	Geo. E. Norris, Brockton, Mass.	The Burleigh Lith. Est., Troy, New York	20×33½
265	Amesbury 1914	(T. M. Fowler Map Coll. 62)	Hughes & Bailey, New York	[Meriden Gravure Co., Meriden, Conn.]	21×29½
266	Amherst 1886		L. R. Burleigh, Troy, New York	The Burleigh Lith. Est., Troy, New York	18×30
267	Ashburnham 1886	L. R. Burleigh, Troy, New York	L. R. Burleigh, Troy, New York		13×20½
268	Ashland 1878	O. H. Bailey & J. C. Hazen, Boston	O. H. Bailey & J. C. Hazen, Boston		20×24½
269	Athol 1887	L. R. Burleigh, Troy, New York	L. R. Burleigh, Troy, New York	L. R. Burleigh, Troy, New York	17½×24½
270	Ayer 1886		L. R. Burleigh, Troy, New York		13×23½
271	Baldwinville 1886		L. R. Burleigh, Troy, New York	Beck & Pauli, Lith., Milwaukee, Wisconsin	13×24½
272	Beverly Farms, 1886		O. W. Walker, Boston		16½×30½

No.	City and Date	Artist	Publisher	Lithographer or Printer	Map Size (Inches)
273	Boston 1870	F. Fuchs	John Weik, Philadelphia	New England Lith. Co., Boston	28½×36½
274	Boston [187–?]	T. Sulman			13×19½
275	Boston, 1873	Parsons & Atwater	Currier & Ives, New York		22½×33
276	Boston, 1877	J. Bachmann	L. Prang & Co.	J. Bachmann	20×25
277	Boston 1879		O. H. Bailey & J. C. Hazen, Boston	Armstrong & Co., Riverside Press, Cambridge	29×44
278	Boston 1880	H. H. Rowley & Co., Hartford, Conn.	H. H. Rowley & Co., Hartford, Conn.	Beck & Pauli, Milwaukee, Wisconsin	33½×54½
279	Boston 1899	E. A. Downs, Boston [A. E. Downs]	E. A. Downs, Boston [A. E. Downs]	Geo. H. Walker & Co., Boston	25×38
280	Boston 1905	Bert Poole	F. D. Nichols Co., Boston	A. W. Elson & Co., Boston	22×30
281	Boston Highlands 1888	Favour	O. H. Bailey & Co.		31×41
282	Brockton 1882	A. F. Poole	J. J. Stoner, Madison, Wisconsin	Beck & Pauli, Lith., Milwaukee, Wisconsin	26×39
283	Canton 1918		Hughes & Bailey, Boston	[Meriden Gravure Co., Meriden, Conn.]	26×36
283A	Clinton 1876	O. H. Bailey & Co.	O. H. Bailey & Co.	J. Knauber & Co.; C. H. Vogt	8×10 photograph
284	Dalton, 1884	L. R. Burleigh, Troy, N.Y.	L. R. Burleigh, Troy, N.Y.	Beck & Pauli, Litho., Milwaukee, Wis.	15×30
285	East Boston 1879	O. H. Bailey & Co., Boston	O. H. Bailey & Co., Boston		21×24
286	East Douglas 1886	L. R. Burleigh, Troy, New York		C. H. Vogt, Lith., The Burleigh Lith. Est., Troy, New York	15×24

No.	City and Date	Artist	Publisher	Lithographer or Printer	Map Size (Inches)
287	East Pepperell 1886	L. R. Burleigh, Troy, New York		C. H. Vogt, Lith.	15×21
288	East Walpole 1898	The Bert Poole Co., Boston	The Bert Poole Co., Boston		15×22½
289	Edgartown [1886]			Geo. H. Walker & Co., **Boston**	13×19
290	Fall River 1877	O. H. Bailey & J. C. Hazen, Boston	O. H. Bailey & J. C. Hazen, Boston	C. H. Vogt, Lith., Milwaukee; J. Knauber & Co.	27×42
291	Fitchburg 1882	L. R. Burleigh, Troy, New York	L. R. Burleigh, Troy, New York	C. H. Vogt, Lith., Cleveland, Ohio	22×31½
292	Fitchburg 1915	T. M. Fowler (T. M. Fowler Map Coll. 66)	Hughes & Bailey, New York	[Meriden Gravure Co., **Meriden, Conn.**]	24×35
293	Graniteville 1886	[C.] Fausel	L. R. Burleigh, Troy, New York	The Burleigh Lith. Est., Troy, New **York**	15×22
294	Great Barrington 1884	L. R. Burleigh, Troy, New York	L. R. Burleigh, Troy, New York	Beck & Pauli, Lith., Milwaukee, **Wisconsin**	17½×30
295	Groton 1886		L. R. Burleigh, Troy, New York	The Burleigh Lith. Est., Troy, New **York**	16×24
296	Haverhill 1893		O. H. Bailey & Co., Boston	O. H. Bailey & Co., Boston	25×36
297	Haverhill 1914	Fowler & Downs	Hughes & Bailey	[Franklin Engraving Co., & Federal Engraving Co., Boston, Mass.]	28×31
298	Haydenville 1886		L. R. Burleigh	Northern Lith. Co., Troy, New **York**	13×20½
299	Hingham and South Hingham, 1885	A. F. Poole and C. E. Jörgensen	A. F. Poole, Brockton, Mass.	Geo. H. Walker & Co., Boston	24½×33
300	Hinsdale 1887	L. R. Burleigh, Troy, New York	L. R. Burleigh, Troy, New York	C. H. Vogt, Cleveland; **Burleigh Lith. Est.,** Troy, New York	14×22

36

No.	City and Date	Artist	Publisher	Lithographer or Printer	Map Size (Inches)
301	Holyoke and South Hadley Falls 1881	A. F. Poole	J. J. Stoner, Madison, Wisconsin	Beck & Pauli, Lith., Milwaukee, Wisconsin	27×38
302	Hopedale 1899	The Bert Poole Co., Boston	The Bert Poole Co., Boston		16×22½
303	Housatonic 1890	L. R. Burleigh, Troy, New York	L. R. Burleigh, Troy, New York		17×23
304	Huntington 1886	L. R. Burleigh, Troy, New York		The Burleigh Lith. Est., Troy, New York	13×21
304A	Lawrence 1876	H. H. Bailey & J. C. Hazen	H. H. Bailey & J. C. Hazen	J. Knauber & Co.; C. H. Vogt	8×10 photograph
305	Leominster 1886	L. R. Burleigh, Troy, New York	L. R. Burleigh, Troy, New York	Burleigh Lith. Est., Troy, New York	16½×29½
305A	Lowell 1876	H. H. Bailey & J. C. Hazen	H. H. Bailey & J. C. Hazen	J. Knauber & Co.; C. H. Vogt	8×10 photograph
306	Lynn 1820	Wm. T. Oliver (Drawn in 1874)	Wm. T. Oliver		6×16
307	Lynn 1881		C. A. Shaw & H. J. Hutchinson	Armstrong & Co., Lith., Boston	27×39
308	Marblehead Shore 1886		O. W. Walker, Boston		17½×30½
309	Maynard 1879	O. H. Bailey & J. C. Hazen, Boston	O. H. Bailey & J. C. Hazen, Boston		22×26
310	Merrimac 1889	Geo. E. Norris, Brockton, Mass.	Geo. E. Norris, Brockton, Mass.		16×27
311	Nantasket Beach 1879	R. P. Mallory	George H. Walker & Co.		17×25½
312	Nantucket 1881 (Inset of Siasconset)		J. J. Stoner, Madison, Wis.	Beck & Pauli, Lith., Milwaukee, Wis.	20×28½

No.	City and Date	Artist	Publisher	Lithographer or Printer	Map Size (Inches)
313	North Attleborough 1878	O. H. Bailey & J. C. Hazen, Boston	O. H. Bailey & J. C. Hazen, Boston	C. H. Vogt, Lith.	22×27
314	North Billerica 1887	L. R. Burleigh, Troy, New York	L. R. Burleigh, Troy, New York	The Burleigh Lith. Est., Troy, New York	15×24
314A	Northboro 1887	Geo. E. Norris, Brockton, Mass.	Geo. E. Norris, Brockton, Mass.	Burleigh Litho. Establishment, Troy, N.Y.	8×10 photograph
315	North Bridgewater 1844	A. F. Poole (Drawn in 1882)	J. J. Stoner, Madison, Wisconsin	Beck & Pauli, Lith., Milwaukee, Wisconsin	12×17
316	North Leominster 1887	L. R. Burleigh	L. R. Burleigh	Burleigh Lith. Est., Troy, New York	17×27
317	Oak Bluffs 1890 [Formerly Cottage City]			Robert A. Welcke, Lith., New York	20×25
318	Peabody 1877	O. H. Bailey & J. C. Hazen, Boston	O. H. Bailey & J. C. Hazen, Boston	J. Knauber & Co., Milwaukee, Wisconsin	20½×26
318A	Plymouth 1882		O. H. Bailey & Co., Boston		8×10 photograph
319	Provincetown 1877		F. K. Rogers, Boston		17×26
320	Provincetown 1910		Walker Lith. & Pub. Co., Boston	Walker Lith. & Pub. Co., Boston	Positive & Negative Photostatic Copies, each 11×17½
321	Quincy 1877	E. Whitefield	E. Whitefield		20×33
322	South Acton 1886		L. R. Burleigh	The Burleigh Lith. Est., Troy, New York	11×22
323	South Weymouth 1885	C. E. Jörgensen	A. F. Poole & Co., Brockton, Mass.	Geo. H. Walker & Co., Boston	20×25½
324	Spencer 1877	O. H. Bailey & J. C. Hazen, Boston	O. H. Bailey & J. C. Hazen, Boston		20×24½

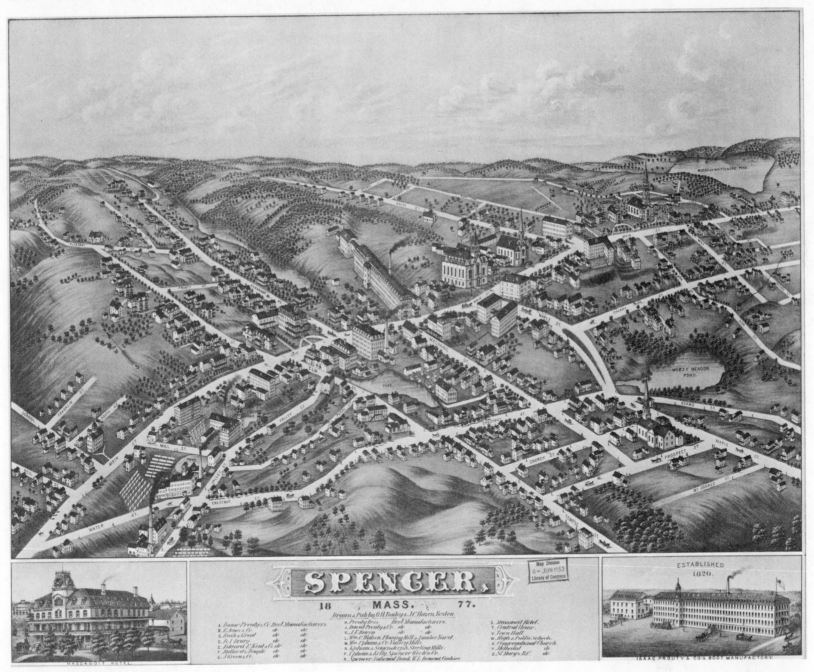

SPENCER,

18   MASS.   77.

Drawn & Pub. by O. H. Bailey & J. C. Hazen, Boston.

ESTABLISHED
1820.

MASSASOIT HOTEL.

ISAAC PROUTY & CO.'S BOOT MANUFACTORY.

A. Isaac Prouty & Co. Boot Manufacturers
B. E. Jones & Co.   do   do
C. Bush & Grout   do   do
D. D. J. Henry   do   do
E. Edward E. Kent & Co.   do   do
F. Bullard & Temple   do   do
G. J. Green & Co.   do   do

H. Prouty Bros.   Boot Manufacturers.
I. David Prouty & Co.   do   do
K. J. E. Bacon   do   do
L. Wm. C. Watson Planing Mill & Lumber Yard.
M. Wm. Upham & Co. Valley Mills.
N. Graham & Sugden & Co. Sterling Mills.
P. Upham & Kelly, Spencer Woolen Co.
R. Spencer National Bank, W. L. Demond Cashier.

S. Massasoit Hotel.
T. Central House.
V. Town Hall.
W. High & Public Schools.
X. Congregational Church
Y. Methodist   do
Z. St. Mary's R. C.   do

39

No.	City and Date	Artist	Publisher	Lithographer or Printer	Map Size (Inches)
325	Springfield 1875		O. H. Bailey & Co.		27½×35
326	Uxbridge 1880		E. H. Bigelow, Framingham, Massachusetts	Beck & Pauli, Milwaukee, Wisconsin	23½×24½
326A	Ware 1878		J. L. Galt & Co.	Beck & Pauli, Milwaukee, Wis.	8×10 photograph
327	Wareham and Onset Bay Grove, 1885		O. W. Walker	Geo. H. Walker & Co., Boston	18×24
328	Westford 1886		L. R. Burleigh	The Burleigh Lith. Est., Troy, New York	12×20
329	Williamstown 1889	L. R. Burleigh	L. R. Burleigh	The Burleigh Lith. Est., Troy, New York	19×29
330	Winchester 1898	Robbins	Robbins & Enrich	Heliotype Co., Boston	18×26
331	Winthrop 1894		Bert [A. F.] Poole		15×24½

Michigan

No.	City and Date	Artist	Publisher	Lithographer or Printer	Map Size (Inches)
332	Adrian 1866	A. Ruger, Battle Creek, Mich.	A. Ruger, Battle Creek, Mich.	Chicago Lith. Co., Chicago	22×34
333	Albion [1868]	A. Ruger, Battle Creek, Mich.	A. Ruger, Battle Creek, Mich.	Chicago Lith. Co.	19¼×28
334	Ann Arbor 1880	[A. Ruger]	J. J. Stoner, Madison, Wisconsin	Beck & Pauli, Lith., Milwaukee, Wisconsin	14¾×27
335	Battle Creek [1869]	A. Ruger, Battle Creek, Mich.	A. Ruger, Battle Creek, Mich.		12¾×20½
336	Battle Creek [1870?]	A. Ruger, Battle Creek, Mich.	A. Ruger, Battle Creek, Mich.		21½×28
337	Battle Creek [188–?]				26×41½

No.	City and Date	Artist	Publisher	Lithographer or Printer	Map Size (Inches)
338	Bay City, Portsmouth, Wenona & Salzburg 1867	A. Ruger		Chicago Lith. Co.	20×28½
339	Benton Harbor 1889	C. J. Pauli & Co., Milwaukee, Wis.	C. J. Pauli & Co., Milwaukee, Wis.		23×29
340	Bessemer 1886		Norris, Wellge & Co., Milwaukee, Wisconsin	Beck & Pauli, Lith., Milwaukee, Wisconsin	10×16¾
341	Coldwater [1868?]	A. Ruger, Battle Creek, Mich.	A. Ruger, Battle Creek, Mich.	Chicago Litho. Co.	19×28½
342	Detroit 1889			The Calvert Lith. Co., Detroit	11½×19½
343	Detroit 1818 & 1906		Hurd Wheeler Co., Detroit		Photographic print 5½×9½
344	Fenton 1880	Jos. Warner	J. J. Stoner, Madison, Wisconsin		Photographic print 8×10
345	Flint 1867	A. Ruger, Battle Creek, Mich.	A. Ruger, Battle Creek, Mich.		Photographic print 16×20
346	Flint 1880				Photographic print 15×20
347	Flint 1890	C. J. Pauli, Milwaukee	C. J. Pauli, Milwaukee		Photographic print 14×20
348	Grand Haven 1868	A. Ruger	E. S. Glover	Merchant's Lith. Co., Chicago	16¾×24
349	Grand Haven 1874		J. J. Stoner, Madison, Wisconsin	Chas. Shober & Co., Props., Chicago Lith. Co.	18×24
350	Grand Rapids 1868	A. Ruger		Chicago Litho. Co.	22½×34½
351	Hillsdale 1866	A. Ruger, Battle Creek, Mich.	A. Ruger, Battle Creek, Mich.	Chicago Litho. Co.	19½×28
352	Hudson 1868	A. Ruger	E. S. Glover	Chicago Litho. Co.	17½×23½

Bay City, Mich., 1867. Drawn by Albert Ruger.

No.	City and Date	Artist	Publisher	Lithographer or Printer	Map Size (Inches)
353	Ionia 1868	A. Ruger		Chicago Litho. Co.	22½×28
354	Ironwood 1886	H. Wellge	Norris, Wellge & Co., Milwaukee, Wisconsin	Beck & Pauli, Litho., Milwaukee, Wisconsin	9½×18
355	Jackson [1868]	A. Ruger, Battle Creek, Mich.	A. Ruger, Battle Creek, Mich.	Chicago Litho. Co.	20½×33¾
356	Jackson 1881	A. Ruger	J. J. Stoner, Madison, Wisconsin	Beck & Pauli, Milwaukee, Wisconsin	15¼×30½
357	Kalamazoo 1874	[Albert Ruger]	J. J. Stoner, Madison, Wisconsin	Chas. Shober & Co., Chicago Lith. Co.	20½×28¼
358	Kalamazoo 1883	H. Wellge & A. F. Poole	J. J. Stoner, Madison, Wisconsin	Beck & Pauli, Milwaukee, Wisconsin	16¾×28¼
359	Lansing 1866	A. Ruger, Battle Creek, Mich.	A. Ruger, Battle Creek, Mich.	Chicago Litho. Co.	22×28½
360	Marquette 1897 (Inset Marquette 1849)				23×41½
361	Marshall [1868?]	A. Ruger, Battle Creek, Mich.	A. Ruger, Battle Creek, Mich.	Chicago Lith. Co.	19×28
362	Monroe 1866	A. Ruger, Battle Creek, Mich.	A. Ruger, Battle Creek, Mich.	Chicago Lith. Co.	19×27½
363	Mt. Clemens 1881		J. J. Stoner, Madison, Wisconsin	Beck & Pauli, Lith., Milwaukee, Wisconsin	12½×22
364	Muskegon 1868	A. Ruger		Chicago Lith. Co.	19¼×27¾
365	Muskegon 1874	[Albert Ruger]		Chas. Shober & Co., Chicago Lith. Co.	18×26
366	Muskegon 1889	E. S. Glover	A. J. Little	Shober-Carqueville Lith. Co., Chicago	21×37¼
367	Negaunee 1871	H. H. Bailey		C. H. Vogt, Lith.; Milwaukee Lith. & Engr. Co.	16½×24
368	Niles [1868?]	A. Ruger, Battle Creek, Mich.	A. Ruger, Battle Creek, Mich.	Chicago Lith. Co.	21×28

No.	City and Date	Artist	Publisher	Lithographer or Printer	Map Size (Inches)
369	Pontiac 1867	A. Ruger, Battle Creek, Mich.	A. Ruger, Battle Creek, Mich.	Chicago Lith. Co.	18¼×28½
370	Port Huron & Gratiot, Michigan 1867 (with Sarnia & Port Edwards, Ontario)	A. Ruger, Battle Creek, Mich.	A. Ruger, Battle Creek, Mich.	Chicago Lith. Co.	19½×28½
371	Port Huron 1894	C. J. Pauli, Milwaukee, Wis.	C. J. Pauli, Milwaukee, Wis.		20½×39
372	Romeo 1868	A. Ruger	E. S. Glover	Chicago Lith. Co.	17×24½
373	Saginaw 1867	A. Ruger		Chicago Lith. Co.	20¼×28¼
374	Saginaw & East Saginaw 1887		O. H. Bailey & Co., Boston	O. H. Bailey & Co., Boston	5½×8½
375	Saint Clair 1868	A. Ruger	E. S. Glover	Chicago Lith. Co.	16¾×23½
376	Saint Johns 1868	A. Ruger		Chicago Lith. Co.	16×24
377	Saranac 1910		H. Peake		Photographic print, 10×16
378	Tecumseh 1868	A. Ruger	E. S. Glover	Chicago Lith. Co.	17¼×23¼
379	Wyandotte 1896	T. M. Fowler, Morrisville, Pa. (T. M. Fowler Map Coll. 69)	T. M. Fowler & James B. Moyer		23×32¼
380	Ypsilanti [1868?]	A. Ruger, Battle Creek, Mich.	A. Ruger, Battle Creek, Mich.	Chicago Lith. Co.	20½×28

Minnesota

381	Anoka 1869	A. Ruger		Merchant's Lith. Co.	17½×20

No.	City and Date	Artist	Publisher	Lithographer or Printer	Map Size (Inches)
382	Appleton 1874 [In Alfred T. Andreas, *An Illustrated Historical Atlas of the State of Minnesota* (Chicago, 1874), p. 83]				5×6
383	Austin 1870		Ruger & Stoner, Madison, Wisconsin	Chicago Lith. Co., Chicago	17×20
384	Brainerd 1914		Brainerd Townsite Co., Duluth	McCoy Duluth Photo-Engraving Co., Duluth, Minnesota	20×26½
385	Duluth 1883	H. Wellge	J. J. Stoner, Madison, Wisconsin	Beck & Pauli Lith. Co., Milwaukee, Wisconsin	16×40

Activity in the harbor predominates in this 1883 view of Duluth, Minn. Drawn by Henry Wellge; published by J. J. Stoner, Madison, Wis.

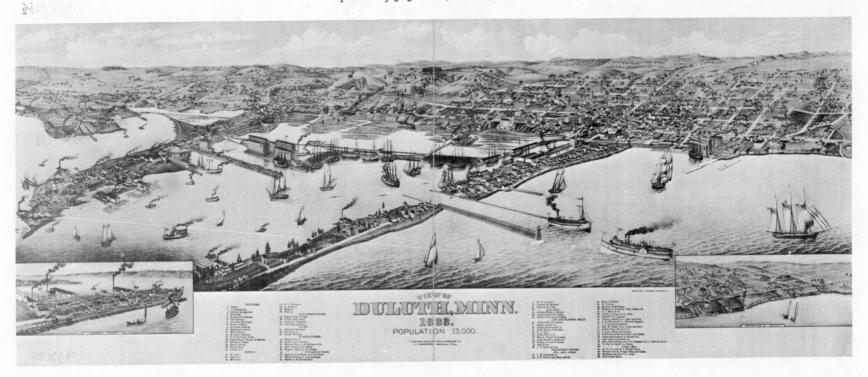

45

No.	City and Date	Artist	Publisher	Lithographer or Printer	Map Size (Inches)
386	Duluth 1887	H. Wellge, Milwaukee, Wis.	The Duluth News Co.	Beck & Pauli Lith. Co., Milwaukee, Wisconsin	22×41
387	Faribault 1869	Prof. A. Ruger		Merchant's Lith. Co., Chicago	21×22½
388	Granite Falls 1874 [In Alfred T. Andreas, *An Illustrated Historical Atlas of the State of Minnesota* (Chicago, 1874), p. 86]				7×12
389	Hastings 1867	A. Ruger		Chicago Lith. Co., Chicago	20×24
390	Lake City 1867	A. Ruger		Chicago Lith. Co., Chicago	19×24
391	Luverne 1883	H. Brosius	J. J. Stoner, Madison, Wisconsin; *Rock Co. Herald*	Beck & Pauli, Milwaukee, Wisconsin	14×21½
392	Mankato 1870	[Albert Ruger]	Ruger & Stoner, Madison, Wis.	Merchants Lithographing Co., Chicago	21×26
393	Minneapolis & Saint Anthony 1867	A. Ruger		Chicago Lith. Co., Chicago	22½×28
394	Minneapolis, 1873	A. Hageboeck, Davenport, Iowa	A. Hageboeck, Davenport, Iowa	A. Hageboeck, Davenport, Iowa	7½×24½
395	Minneapolis 1879	A. Ruger	J. J. Stoner, Madison, Wisconsin	Beck & Pauli, Lith., Milwaukee, Wisconsin	20½×32½
396	Minneapolis 1885	W. V. Herancourt	J. Monasch, Minneapolis		27½×40½
397	Minneapolis 1891	Frank Pezolt	A. M. Smith	E. G. Christoph Lith. Co., Chicago	29×41
398	Minneapolis 1891	Frank Pezolt	A. M. Smith		15½×21½

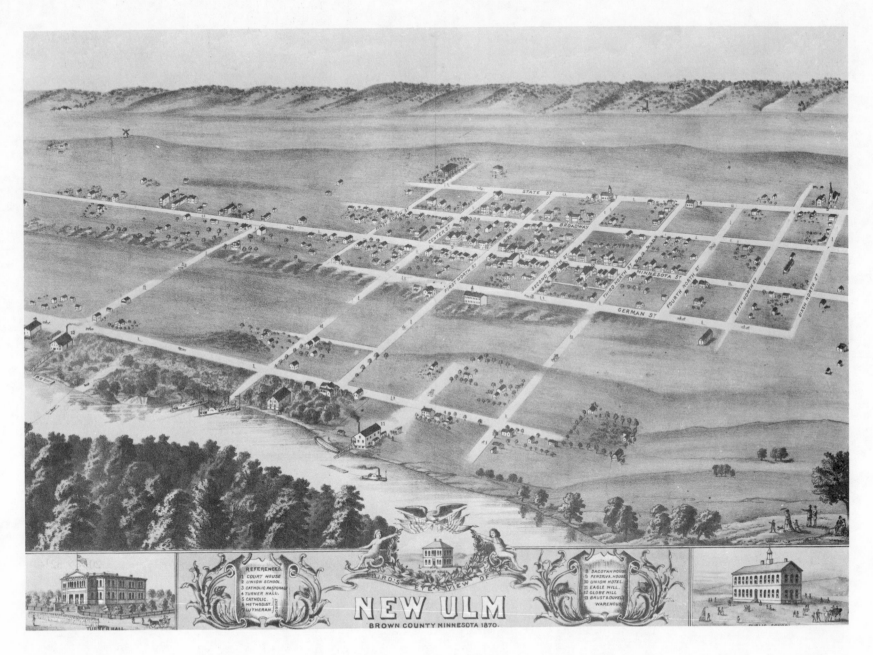

REFERENCES
1 COURT HOUSE
2 UNION SCHOOL
3 CATHOLIC PASTORAGE
4 TURNER HALL
5 CATHOLIC
6 METHODIST CHURCHES
7 LUTHERAN

8 DACOTAH HOUSE
9 PERSTVA. HOUSE
10 UNION HOTEL
11 EAGLE MILL
12 GLOBE MILL
13 BRUST & DUYEL WAREHOUSE

BIRD'S EYE VIEW OF

NEW ULM
BROWN COUNTY MINNESOTA 1870.

TURNER HALL

PUBLIC SCHOOL

New Ulm, Minn., 1870. Drawn by Albert Ruger; published by A. Ruger & Stoner, Madison, Wis.

No.	City and Date	Artist	Publisher	Lithographer or Printer	Map Size (Inches)
399	Montevideo 1874 [In Alfred T. Andreas, *An Illustrated Historical Atlas of the State of Minnesota* (Chicago, 1874), p. 86]				7½×12
400	New Ulm 1870	A. Ruger	A. Ruger & Stoner, Madison, Wisconsin	Chicago Lith. Co., Chicago	15½×20½
401	Northfield 1869		Ruger & Stoner, Madison, Wisconsin	Chicago Lith. Co., Chicago	17×20
402	Owatonna 1870		Ruger & Stoner, Madison, Wisconsin	Merchant's Lith. Co., Chicago	18×20½
403	Preston 1874 [In Alfred T. Andreas, *An Illustrated Historical Atlas of the State of Minnesota* (Chicago, 1874), p. 188]	E. S. Moore			7½×12
404	Redwing 1868	A. Ruger		Robert Teufel, Chicago	18½×24½
405	Rochester 1869		Ruger & Stoner, Madison, Wisconsin	Merchant's Lith. Co., Chicago	20½×22
406	Saint Cloud 1869	A. Ruger		Merchant's Lith. Co., Chicago	21×24
407	St. Paul 1867	A. Ruger		Chicago Lith. Co., Chicago	22½×28
408	St. Paul 1873	A. Hageboeck, Davenport, Iowa	A. Hageboeck, Davenport, Iowa	A. Hageboeck, Davenport, Iowa	7½×24½
409	St. Paul [1874]	Hoffman	George Ellsbury & Vernon Green		16½×29½
410	St. Paul 1893		Brown, Tracy & Co.		8×10½

No.	City and Date	Artist	Publisher	Lithographer or Printer	Map Size (Inches)
411	St. Paul 1906		Robert M. Saint, St. Paul		16½×30½
412	Saint Peter 1870		Ruger & Stoner, Madison, Wisconsin	Merchant's Lith. Co. Chicago	17½×20½
413	Shakopee 1869	A. Ruger & Stoner, Madison, Wis.		Chicago Lith. Co., Chicago	16×20½
414	Stillwater 1870	A. Ruger		Merchant's Lith. Co., Chicago	20½×22½
415	Winona 1867	A. Ruger		Chicago Lith. Co., Chicago	22½×28½
416	Winona 1874		George H. Ellsbury & Vernon Green	Chas. Shober & Co., Chicago Lith. Co.	18×28½
417	Winona 1889	C. J. Pauli	C. J. Pauli & Co., Milwaukee, Wisconsin		18×40

Missouri

No.	City and Date	Artist	Publisher	Lithographer or Printer	Map Size (Inches)
418	Brookfield 1869	A. Ruger			17×20½
419	California 1869	A. Ruger			17×18
420	Carthage 1891	T. M. Fowler, Morrisville, Pa. (T. M. Fowler Map Coll. 5)	T. M. Fowler & James B. Moyer		16¼×32
421	Chillicothe 1869	A. Ruger			21×26
422	Columbia 1869	A. Ruger			17½×22
423	Hannibal 1869	A. Ruger			22½×26
424	Hermann 1869	A. Ruger			14×16½
425	Holden 1869	A. Ruger			11×12
426	Independence 1868	A. Ruger			21½×26½

No.	City and Date	Artist	Publisher	Lithographer or Printer	Map Size (Inches)
427	Jefferson City 1869	A. Ruger			20×26
428	Kansas City 1869 (Inset Kansas City 1855)	A. Ruger	Ruger & Stoner, Madison, Wisconsin	Merchant's Lith. Co., Chicago	22×28
429	Kansas City (West Bottoms) 1895		Augustus Koch		32½×49½
430	Lexington 1869	A. Ruger			20½×26
431	Macon City 1869	A. Ruger			20½×26
432	Mexico 1869	A. Ruger			20×26
433	Pacific 1869 (Formerly Franklin)	A. Ruger			10×12
434	Palmyra 1869	A. Ruger			20×26
435	Pleasant Hill 1869	A. Ruger			14×18
436	Saint Charles 1869	A. Ruger			20½×26
437	Saint Joseph 1868	A. Ruger		Merchant's Lith. Co., Chicago	22½×28
438	St. Louis [1848]	J. M. Kershaw, St. Louis	J. M. Kershaw, St. Louis	J. M. Kershaw, St. Louis	8½×10½
439	St. Louis 1875	Camille N. Dry	Compton & Co. (1876)	St. Louis Globe-Democrat Job Printing Co.	Atlas in 110 plates, each plate 13×18½
440	St. Louis 1784 & 1884			J. E. Lawton Printing Co.	18½×26
441	St. Louis 1893	Fred Graf	Fred Graf, St. Louis	Fred Graf, St. Louis	25½×39¼
442	St. Louis 1894	Chas. Juehne	Chas. Juehne		18×24
443	St. Louis 1895		Chas. Juehne	Chas. Juehne	23×40

No.	City and Date	Artist	Publisher	Lithographer or Printer	Map Size (Inches)
444	St. Louis 1896	Fred Graf, St. Louis	Graf Eng. Co., St. Louis		26×40½
445	St. Louis 1896	Chas. Juehne	Chas. Juehne	Chas. Juehne	23½×40
446	St. Louis 1897				8½×9½
447	St. Louis (Wholesale & Office District) 1904	Charles Juehne	Charles Juehne		5×10½
448	St. Louis 1907	Fred Graf	Fred Graf Engraving Co., St. Louis		19½×24½
449	Sedalia 1869	A. Ruger			21×26½
450	Warrensburg 1869	A. Ruger			16×20
451	Washington 1869	A. Ruger			21×26

Montana

No.	City and Date	Artist	Publisher	Lithographer or Printer	Map Size (Inches)
452	Billings 1904	H. Wellge	H. Wellge, Milwaukee, Wisconsin		18×28½
453	Butte-City 1884	H. Wellge	J. J. Stoner, Madison, Wisconsin	Beck & Pauli, Lith., Milwaukee, Wisconsin	20×29
454	Great Falls 1891		American Publishing Co., Milwaukee, Wisconsin		24×33
455	Helena 1875	E. S. Glover	C. K. Wells, Helena, Montana Territory	A. L. Bancroft & Co., San Francisco, California	20½×27
456	Helena 1883		J. J. Stoner, Milwaukee, Wisconsin	Beck & Pauli, Lith., Milwaukee, Wisconsin	17×26
457	Helena 1890		American Publishing Co., Milwaukee, Wisconsin		27×40
458	Livingston 1883		J. J. Stoner, Madison, Wisconsin	Beck & Pauli, Lith., Milwaukee, Wisconsin	16×22½

No.	City and Date	Artist	Publisher	Lithographer or Printer	Map Size (Inches)
459	Miles City 1883		J. J. Stoner, Madison, Wisconsin	Beck & Pauli, Lith., Milwaukee, Wisconsin	14×22
460	Missoula 1884	H. Wellge	J. J. Stoner, Madison, Wisconsin	Beck & Pauli, Lith., Milwaukee, Wisconsin	16×24
461	Missoula 1891		American Publishing Co., Milwaukee, Wisconsin		22×33½

Nebraska

No.	City and Date	Artist	Publisher	Lithographer or Printer	Map Size (Inches)
462	Kearney 1889	H. Wellge	American Publishing Co., Milwaukee, Wisconsin		24×36½
463	Lincoln 1880	Augustus Koch	Reproduced in 1970 by Historic Urban Plans, Ithaca, New York	Ramsey, Millett & Hudson, Kansas City, Mo.	20¼×25½
464	Lincoln 1889	H. Wellge	American Publishing Co., Milwaukee, Wisconsin		22½×32
465	Nebraska City 1868	A. Ruger		Merchant's Lith. Co., Chicago	21×26
466	Norfolk 1889 (Inset Norfolk 1884)	H. Wellge	American Publishing Co., Milwaukee, Wisconsin		18×24½
467	Omaha 1868	A. Ruger		Chicago Lith. Co.	22½×28
467A	Omaha 1876	Augustus Koch		Charles Shober & Co., Chicago Litho'g. Co.	8×10 photograph
468	Omaha 1906	Edw. J. Austen	Bee Publishing Co.		17×32

Nevada

No.	City and Date	Artist	Publisher	Lithographer or Printer	Map Size (Inches)
468A	Reno [1890]		C. C. Powning; Reproduced by Historic Urban Plans, Ithaca, New York	H. S. Crocker & Co.	16½×23
469	Virginia City 1875	Augustus Koch		Britton, Rey & Co., San Francisco	24×28½

No.	City and Date	Artist	Publisher	Lithographer or Printer	Map Size (Inches)
	New Hampshire				
470	Ashland 1883		Poole & Norris, Brockton, Massachusetts	Beck & Pauli, Milwaukee, Wisconsin	15½×14½
471	Bethlehem 1883	A. F. Poole	Poole & Norris, Brockton, Massachusetts	Beck & Pauli, Milwaukee, Wisconsin	16×20
472	Claremont 1877	A. Ruger		Shober & Carqueville Lith. Co., Chicago	20×24½
473	Concord 1899		Bert Poole		22½×28
474	Concord 1899		G. M. Clough, Boston		22½×28
475	Dover 1877	A. Ruger		D. Bremner & Co., Milwaukee, Wisconsin	23½×25
476	Exeter 1884	H. Wellge	Norris & Wellge, Brockton, Massachusetts		17½×21½
477	Exeter 1896		A. W. Moore Co., Boston	A. W. Moore, Co., Boston	27½×32
478	Franklin and Franklin Falls 1884 (Inset Franklin Falls 1856)	H. Wellge	Norris & Wellge, Brockton, Massachusetts		17×20
479	Great Falls, New Hampshire and Berwick, Maine 1877	A. Ruger	J. J. Stoner, Madison, Wisconsin	C. H. Vogt & Co., Milwaukee	23×24
480	Greenville 1886 (View of Mason Village 1847)		L. R. Burleigh, Troy, N.Y.	The Burleigh Lith. Establishment, Troy, N.Y.	13½×20
481	Hillsborough-Bridge 1884	H. W. [H. Wellge]	Norris & Wellge, Brockton, Massachusetts		15×18
482	Hinsdale [1886]	L. R. Burleigh, Troy, New York	L. R. Burleigh, Troy, New York	C. H. Vogt & Son, Cleveland, Ohio	14×24½
483	Laconia 1883		Poole & Norris, Brockton, Massachusetts	Beck & Pauli, Milwaukee, Wisconsin	17×21

No.	City and Date	Artist	Publisher	Lithographer or Printer	Map Size (Inches)
484	Lake Village 1883		Poole & Norris, Brockton, Massachusetts	Beck & Pauli, Milwaukee, Wisconsin	13×19
485	Littleton 1883	A. Poole	Poole & Norris, Brockton, Massachusetts	Beck & Pauli, Milwaukee, Wisconsin	19×21½
486	Meredith Village 1889	George E. Norris, Brockton, Massachusetts	George E. Norris, Brockton, Massachusetts	The Burleigh Lith. Est., Troy, New York	16×25
487	Lancaster 1883	A. F. Poole	Poole & Norris, Brockton, Massachusetts	Beck & Pauli, Milwaukee, Wisconsin	16×19½
488	Milford 1886	C. H. Vogt; L. R. Burleigh, Troy, New York	L. R. Burleigh, Troy, New York		16×24½
489	Penacook [1887]	L. R. Burleigh, Troy, New York	L. R. Burleigh, Troy, New York		16×24½
490	Peterborough 1886 (with South Peterboro & West Peterboro)	L. R. Burleigh, Troy, New York	L. R. Burleigh, Troy, New York	Burleigh Lith. Est.	16½×25
491	Pittsfield 1884		Geo. E. Norris, Brockton, Massachusetts	Beck & Pauli, Milwaukee, Wisconsin	18×24
492	Portsmouth 1877	A. Ruger	[J. J. Stoner, Madison, Wisconsin]	D. Bremner & Co., Milwaukee, Wisconsin	22×26½
493	Rochester 1884 (with Gonic & East Rochester)	H. Wellge	Norris & Wellge, Brockton, Massachusetts		17×20
494	Salmon Falls 1877			Jos. B. Richards & Co., Boston	10½×12½
495	South New Market 1884		Norris & Wellge, Brockton, Massachusetts		15×18
496	Tilton 1884	H. Wellge	Norris & Wellge, Brockton, Massachusetts		16×20

No.	City and Date	Artist	Publisher	Lithographer or Printer	Map Size (Inches)
497	West Lebanon, New Hampshire & White River Junction, Vermont, 1889	Geo. E. Norris, Brockton, Mass.	Geo. E. Norris, Brockton, Mass.	The Burleigh Lith. Est., Troy, New York	17½×25½
498	Whitefield 1883	A. F. Poole	Poole & Norris, Brockton, Massachusetts	Beck & Pauli, Milwaukee, Wisconsin	16×19
499	Wolfeborough, Lake Winnipesaukee 1889 (with South Wolfboro)	Geo. E. Norris, Brockton, Mass.	Geo. E. Norris, Brockton, Mass.	The Burleigh Lith. Est., Troy, New York	17×25½

New Jersey

No.	City and Date	Artist	Publisher	Lithographer or Printer	Map Size (Inches)
500	Absecon 1924	Rene Cinquin	Hughes & Cinquin, New York	[Meriden Gravure Co., Meriden, Conn.]	25×35
501	Arlington 1907				14½×26
502	Asbury Park & Ocean Grove 1881	T. M. Fowler, Asbury Park, N.J.	T. M. Fowler, Asbury Park, N.J.	Beck & Pauli, Milwaukee, Wisconsin	20×35
503	Asbury Park, Ocean Grove & Vicinity 1897		Landis & Hughes, New York		33×40½
504	Asbury Park 1910	H. M. Pettit	Barton & Spooner Co., New York		7½×9½
505	Atlantic City 1900		Landis & Alsop, Newark		38×55½
506	Atlantic City 1905		Nation Publishing Co., New York		10×24
507	Atlantic City 1908		W. Adickes, Newark, New Jersey		4×7

No.	City and Date	Artist	Publisher	Lithographer or Printer	Map Size (Inches)
508	Atlantic City 1909		Hughes & Bailey, New York		20×38
509	Atlantic City 1910 (c1909)	(T. M. Fowler Map Coll. 6)	Hughes & Bailey, New York		20×42
510	Atlantic Highlands 1894		O. H. Bailey & Co., Boston		23×32
511	Dover 1903	[T. M. Fowler] (T. M. Fowler Map Coll. 7)	Fowler & Bailey, Boston, Mass.		17½×20
512	Egg Harbor City 1865		F. Scheu, Egg Harbor City	Herline & Hensel, Lith., Philadelphia	22×27
513	Egg Harbor City 1924 (Inset Egg Harbor City 1855)	Rene Cinquin	Hughes & Cinquin, Brooklyn, New York	[Meriden Gravure Co., Meriden, Conn.]	20×34½
514	Elizabeth 1898		Landis & Hughes, New York		32×44
515	Garfield 1909	T. M. Fowler, Morrisville, Pa. (T. M. Fowler Map Coll. 8)	T. M. Fowler, Morrisville, Pa.		20×28
516	Hammonton 1926		Hughes & Bailey, Brooklyn, New York	[Stankovits & Co., Brooklyn, New York]	26×31
517	Hoboken 1881		O. H. Bailey, Boston		22½×26
518	Hoboken 1904		Hughes & Bailey, New York		26½×32
519	Maplewood 1910	H. S. Wyllie, Newark			11½×14½
520	Margate City 1925	Rene Cinquin	Hughes & Cinquin, Brooklyn, New York		21×34½
521	Morristown 1899		Landis & Alsop, Newark, New Jersey		33×46

No.	City and Date	Artist	Publisher	Lithographer or Printer	Map Size (Inches)
522	Newark, Harrison, Kearney 1895		T. J. S. Landis, Newark		30×43½
523	Newark 1916		T. J. S. Landis, Newark, New Jersey		23×31
524	New Brunswick 1910		Hughes & Bailey, New York		35×44
525	Plainfield and North Plainfield 1899		Landis & Hughes, New York		31×47½
526	Rutherford 1904		T. J. Hughes, New York		22×27
527	Somers-Point 1925	R. Cinquin	Hughes & Cinquin, Brooklyn, New York	[Meriden Gravure Co., Meriden, Conn.]	25×34
527A	Somerville 1882	T. M. Fowler	Fowler & Evans, Asbury Park, N.J.	Beck & Pauli, Milwaukee, Wis.	15×25
528	Vineland 1885		O. H. Bailey & Co., Boston	O. H. Bailey & Co., Boston	23½×32½
529	Westfield 1929	Rene Cinquin	Hughes & Cinquin, New York	[Meriden Gravure Co., Meriden, Conn.]	27×31
530	Westwood 1924	Rene Cinquin	Hughes & Cinquin, Brooklyn, New York	[Meriden Gravure Co., Meriden, Conn.]	22½×34
531	Woodbury 1886		O. H. Bailey & Co., Boston	O. H. Bailey & Co., Boston	25×32½

New Mexico

No.	City and Date	Artist	Publisher	Lithographer or Printer	Map Size (Inches)
532	Las Vegas 1882		J. J. Stoner, Madison, Wisconsin	Beck & Pauli, Milwaukee, Wisconsin	17×21½
533	Santa Fé 1882	H. Wellge	J. J. Stoner, Madison, Wisconsin	Beck & Pauli, Milwaukee, Wisconsin	13×19

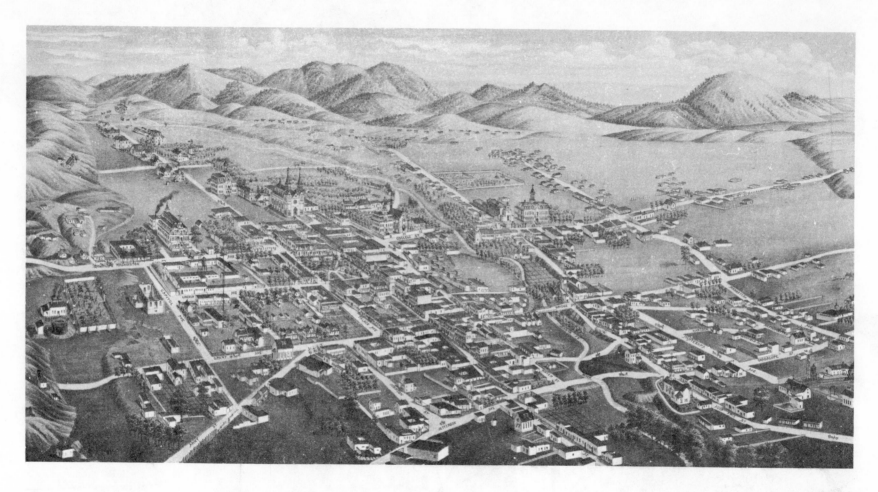

Santa Fé, N. Mex., 1882.   Drawn by Henry Wellge; published by J. J. Stoner, Madison, Wis.

No.	City and Date	Artist	Publisher	Lithographer or Printer	Map Size (Inches)
	New York				
534	Albany 1879	H. H. Rowley & Co., Hartford, Conn.	H. H. Rowley & Co., Hartford, Connecticut	Beck & Pauli, Milwaukee, Wisconsin	30×44½
535	Amityville 1925	Rene Cinquin, New York	Metropolitan Aero-View Co., New York		25×38
536	Antwerp 1888	C. F. [i.e. Fausel]		The Burleigh Lith. Est., Troy, New York	17×24
537	Bainbridge 1889	L. R. Burleigh, Troy, New York	L. R. Burleigh, Troy, New York	The Burleigh Lith. Est., Troy, New York	14½×23½
537A	Bay Side Park [Queens] 1915		North Shore Realty Co., New York		22½×26
538	Binghamton 1901		Landis & Alsop, Newark, New Jersey		In 2 parts, each 40×28½
539	Brewster 1887		The Burleigh Litho. Est., Troy, New York		13×21
540	Bronx 1897 (Vicinity of Grand Concourse)	Wm. W. Klein	Department of Street Improvements, 23rd & 24th Wards	Robert A. Welcke Photo Lith., New York	In 2 parts, each 17×35
541	Brooklyn 1879	C. R. Parsons	Currier & Ives, New York		23×33½
542	Buffalo 1880		E. H. Hutchinson, Buffalo, N.Y.	Maerz Lithographing Co., Buffalo, N.Y.	25×37½
543	Buffalo 1902		Landis & Alsop, Newark, N.J.		41×58½
544	Caledonia 1892		Burleigh Litho. Co., Troy, New York		17×25
545	Cambridge 1886		L. R. Burleigh, Troy, New York	Burleigh Lith. Est., Troy, New York	17×27½

No.	City and Date	Artist	Publisher	Lithographer or Printer	Map Size (Inches)
546	Canastota 1885	L. R. Burleigh, Troy, N.Y. (T. M. Fowler Map Coll. 9)	L. R. Burleigh, Troy, N.Y.	C. H. Vogt & Son, Lith., Cleveland, O.	14½×24
547	Canton 1885	L. R. Burleigh, Troy, New York	L. R. Burleigh, Troy, New York	C. H. Vogt & Son, Cleveland, Ohio	15×24½
548	Carthage 1888	L. R. Burleigh, Troy, New York	L. R. Burleigh, Troy, New York	Burleigh Lith. Est., Troy, New York	18×28
549	Catskill 1889	L. R. Burleigh, Troy, New York	L. R. Burleigh, Troy, New York	The Burleigh Lith. Est., Troy, New York	19×29½
550	Cazenovia 1890		L. R. Burleigh, Troy, New York	Burleigh Lith. Est., Troy, New York	18×31
551	Chatham 1886		L. R. Burleigh, Troy, New York	The Burleigh Lith. Est., Troy, New York	14×29½
552	Clinton 1885	L. R. Burleigh, Troy, New York	L. R. Burleigh, Troy, New York	Beck & Pauli, Lith., Milwaukee, Wisconsin	15×26
553	Cooperstown 1890		L. R. Burleigh, Troy, New York	Burleigh Lith. Est., Troy, New York	17×28½
554	Corinth and Palmer Falls 1888	L. R. Burleigh, Troy, New York	L. R. Burleigh, Troy, New York	The Burleigh Lith. Est., Troy, New York	17×27
555	Delhi 1887	L. R. Burleigh, Troy, New York	L. R. Burleigh, Troy, New York	Burleigh Lith. Est., Troy, New York	15½×20½
556	Deposit 1887	L. R. Burleigh, Troy, New York	L. R. Burleigh, Troy, New York	The Burleigh Lith. Est., Troy, New York	15×24½
557	East Syracuse 1885	L. R. Burleigh, Troy, New York	L. R. Burleigh, Troy, New York	C. H. Vogt & Son, Cleveland, Ohio	12½×25
558	Ellenville 1887	L. R. Burleigh, Troy, New York	L. R. Burleigh, Troy, New York	The Burleigh Lith. Est., Troy, New York	17×27
559	Elmira & Elmira Heights 1901		Landis & Alsop, Newark, New Jersey		In 4 parts, each 18×26

No.	City and Date	Artist	Publisher	Lithographer or Printer	Map Size (Inches)
560	Fairport 1884	L. R. Burleigh, Troy, New York	L. R. Burleigh, Troy, New York	Beck & Pauli, Lith., Milwaukee, Wisconsin	15×24
561	Farmingdale 1925	Rene Cinquin	Metropolitan Aero-View Co., New York		22×34
562	Fishkill-on-the-Hudson 1886	L. R. Burleigh, Troy, New York	L. R. Burleigh, Troy, New York	Burleigh Lith. Est., Troy, New York	17×26
563	Fort Plain & Nelliston 1891		L. R. Burleigh, Troy, New York	Burleigh Lith. Est., Troy, New York	20×27
564	Frankfort 1887	L. R. Burleigh, Troy, New York	L. R. Burleigh, Troy, New York	Burleigh Lith. Est., Troy, New York	17×24
565	Freeport 1909		Hughes & Bailey, New York		21×34½
566	Freeport 1925	R. Cinquin	Metropolitan Aero-View Co., New York		23½×34
567	Glens Falls 1884	L. R. Burleigh, Troy, New York	L. R. Burleigh, Troy, New York	Beck & Pauli, Lith., Milwaukee, Wisconsin	18½×30
568	Gloversville 1875	H. H. Bailey & Co.	H. H. Bailey & Co.	G. W. Lewis, Albany, New York	18½×24
569	Gouverneur 1885	L. R. Burleigh, Troy, New York	L. R. Burleigh, Troy, New York	Beck & Pauli, Litho., Milwaukee, Wisconsin	15×30
570	Granville 1886		L. R. Burleigh, Troy, New York	Beck & Pauli, Litho., Milwaukee, Wisconsin	14×24
571	Hicksville 1925	Rene Cinquin	Metropolitan Aero-View Co., New York		26×36
572	Hoosick Falls 1889	L. R. Burleigh, Troy, New York	L. R. Burleigh, Troy, New York	The Burleigh Lith. Est., Troy, New York	19×31½
573	Hunter 1890		L. R. Burleigh, Troy, New York	Burleigh Lith. Est., Troy, New York	17½×26½
574	Ithaca 1836	H[enry] Walton	Reproduced in 1968 by Historic Urban Plans, Ithaca, New York	Bufford's Lithography, N.Y.	16¼×26¾

No.	City and Date	Artist	Publisher	Lithographer or Printer	Map Size (Inches)
574A	Ithaca 1873		Reproduced in 1972 by Historic Urban Plans, Ithaca, New York		20×25
574B	Ithaca 1882	L. R. Burleigh	Reproduced in 1970 by Historic Urban Plans, Ithaca, New York		20×29
575	Jamestown 1882	H. Brosius & A. F. Poole	J. J. Stoner, Madison, Wisconsin	Beck & Pauli, Litho., Milwaukee, Wisconsin	27½×42
576	Johnsonville 1887	L. R. Burleigh, Troy, New York	L. R. Burleigh, Troy, New York	Burleigh Lith. Est., Troy, New York	12½×22
577	Johnstown 1888	L. R. Burleigh, Troy, New York	L. R. Burleigh, Troy, New York	Burleigh Lith., Troy, New York	17½×29½
578	Keeseville 1887	L. R. Burleigh, Troy, New York	L. R. Burleigh, Troy, New York	Burleigh Lith. Est., Troy, New York	15×24
579	Larchmont 1904		Hughes & Bailey, New York		21×25
580	Le Roy 1892		Burleigh Litho. Co., Troy, New York		19½×30½
581	Lindenhurst 1926	R. Cinquin, New York	Metropolitan Aero-View Co., New York		27×32
582	Lowville 1885	L. R. Burleigh, Troy, New York	L. R. Burleigh, Troy, New York	Beck & Pauli, Litho., Milwaukee, Wisconsin	17×24
583	Luzerne & Hadley 1888	L. R. Burleigh, Troy, New York	L. R. Burleigh, Troy, New York		18×24½
584	Malone 1886	L. R. Burleigh, Troy, New York	L. R. Burleigh, Troy, New York	C. H. Vogt & Son, Cleveland, Ohio	16×30½
585	Matteawan 1886	L. R. Burleigh, Troy, New York	L. R. Burleigh, Troy, New York	Burleigh Lith. Est., Troy, New York	17×23
586	Mechanicville [188?]	L. R. Burleigh, Troy, New York	L. R. Burleigh, Troy, New York	Beck & Pauli, Litho., Milwaukee, Wisconsin	15×25½

No.	City and Date	Artist	Publisher	Lithographer or Printer	Map Size (Inches)
587	Middletown 1887	L. R. Burleigh, Troy, New York	L. R. Burleigh, Troy, New York		18×30½
588	Middletown 1921	[T. M. Fowler] (T. M. Fowler Map Coll. 10)	Hughes & Fowler		23×35
589	Middletown 1922	[T. M. Fowler]	Hughes & Fowler, Brooklyn, New York		26½×36½
590	Middleville 1890		L. R. Burleigh, Troy, New York	Burleigh Lith. Est., Troy, New York	17×23
591	Millerton 1887 (with Irondale)	L. R. Burleigh, Troy, New York	L. R. Burleigh, Troy, New York	The Burleigh Lith. Est., Troy, New York	15×18½

Johnsonville, N.Y., 1887.   Drawn and published by L. R. Burleigh, Troy, N.Y.

No.	City and Date	Artist	Publisher	Lithographer or Printer	Map Size (Inches)
592	Monroe 1923		Hughes & Bailey	[Meriden Gravure Co., Meriden, Conn.]	18×32
593	Newburgh 1900	[T. J. Hughes]			16½×32½
594	Newport 1890		L. R. Burleigh, Troy, New York	Burleigh Lith. Est., Troy, New York	16×25
595	New York 1870		Currier and Ives, New York		22×33
596	New York and Brooklyn 1875	Parsons & Atwater	Currier & Ives		24×33½
597	New York 1876	Parsons & Atwater	Currier & Ives, New York		23½×34
598	New York and Brooklyn 1877	Parsons & Atwater	Currier & Ives, New York		24×33
599	New York 1879	Will L. Taylor	Galt & Hoy, New York	Galt & Hoy, New York	In 4 parts, each 37×21
600	New York 1879	J. W. Williams	Root & Tinker, New York		25½×18
601	New York 1879	J. W. Williams	Root & Tinker		11½×8
602	New York 1884		Currier & Ives, New York		25×35
603	New York 1886	Parsons & Atwater	Currier & Ives, New York		25×34
604	New York 1889	Parsons & Atwater	Currier & Ives, New York		25×34
605	New York 1891	Howard P. Taylor		The Courier Lith. Co., Buffalo, New York	40×28½
606	New York 1892		Currier & Ives, New York		26×36
607	New York & Brooklyn 1892	Parsons & Atwater	Currier & Ives, New York		24½×33½

No.	City and Date	Artist	Publisher	Lithographer or Printer	Map Size (Inches)
608	Niagara Falls 1882	H. Wellge	J. J. Stoner, Madison, Wisconsin	Beck & Pauli, Lith., Milwaukee, Wisconsin	21×29
609	Olean 1882 (Inset of Boardmanville)	H. Brosius	J. J. Stoner, Madison, Wisconsin	Beck & Pauli, Lith., Milwaukee, Wisconsin	26×40
610	Oxford 1888	L. R. Burleigh, Troy, New York	L. R. Burleigh, Troy, New York	The Burleigh Lith. Est., Troy, New York	16½×25
611	Patchogue 1906		Hughes & Bailey, New York		28×33
612	Patchogue 1911		Great South Bay Development Co.	Moessner-Blanchard Art Service, N.Y.	14½×30
613	Pawling 1908	P. H. Smith	W. G. Tice	Knickerbocker Litho. Co., New York	19×25
614	Pearl River 1924	Rene Cinquin	Hughes & Bailey, Brooklyn, New York	[Stankovits & Co., New York, New York]	19×32
615	Peekskill 1911	Fowler & Hughes	Hughes & Bailey, New York	[Consolidated Engraving Co., New York, New York]	25×33
616	Plattsburgh 1877	A. Ruger	J. J. Stoner, Madison, Wisconsin	C. H. Vogt & Co., Milwaukee	23×24½
617	Plattsburgh 1899	C. Fausel		L. R. Burleigh, Lith., Troy, New York	21½×32½
618	Poland 1890		L. R. Burleigh, Troy, New York	Burleigh Lith. Est., Troy, New York	16×23
619	Port Henry 1889	L. R. Burleigh, Troy, New York	L. R. Burleigh, Troy, New York		19×29
620	Port Jervis 1920	[T. M. Fowler] (T. M. Fowler Map Coll. 11)	Hughes & Fowler, Brooklyn, N.Y.		24×32
621	Potsdam 1885	L. R. Burleigh, Troy, New York	L. R. Burleigh, Troy, New York	Beck & Pauli, Litho., Milwaukee, Wisconsin	16×26½
622	Pulaski 1885	L. R. Burleigh, Troy, New York	L. R. Burleigh, Troy, New York	C. H. Vogt & Son, Cleveland	17×24½

Valley Stream, N.Y., 1924, with insets of various buildings and the "North East Section." Drawn by Rene Cinquin; published by Hughes & Cinquin, Brooklyn,

No.	City and Date	Artist	Publisher	Lithographer or Printer	Map Size (Inches)
623	Rhinebeck 1890	L. R. Burleigh, Troy, New York	L. R. Burleigh, Troy, New York		16×25
624	Richfield Springs 1885	L. R. Burleigh, Troy, New York	L. R. Burleigh, Troy, New York	C. H. Vogt & Son, Cleveland	16×26½
625	Rochester 1880	H. H. Rowley & Co., Hartford, Conn.	H. H. Rowley & Co., Hartford, Conn.	Beck & Pauli, Milwaukee, Wisconsin	36×44½
626	Rome 1886	L. R. Burleigh, Troy, New York	L. R. Burleigh, Troy, New York	Beck & Pauli, Litho., Milwaukee, Wisconsin	19×34
627	St. Johnsville 1890		L. R. Burleigh, Troy, New York	Burleigh Lith. Est., Troy, New York	17×23
628	Salem 1889 (Inset of Salem 1789)	L. R. Burleigh, Troy, New York	L. R. Burleigh, Troy, New York	The Burleigh Lith. Est., Troy, New York	19×29½
629	Sandy Hill 1884 (Now called Hudson Falls)	L. R. Burleigh, Troy, New York	L. R. Burleigh, Troy, New York	Beck & Pauli, Litho., Milwaukee, Wisconsin	17½×30½
630	Saratoga Springs 1888	L. R. Burleigh, Troy, New York	L. R. Burleigh, Troy, New York	The Burleigh Lith. Est., Troy, New York	22×34
631	Schaghticoke 1889				16½×22
632	Schuylerville 1889	L. R. Burleigh, Troy, New York	L. R. Burleigh, Troy, New York	The Burleigh Lith. Est., Troy, New York	17×25½
633	Sherburne 1887	L. R. Burleigh, Troy, New York	L. R. Burleigh, Troy, New York	The Burleigh Lith. Est., Troy, New York	15×24½
633A	Shushan 1890		L. R. Burleigh, Troy, N.Y. Reproduced in 1972.	Burleigh Lithographing Establishment, Troy, N.Y.	10×16
634	Sidney 1887	L. R. Burleigh, Troy, New York	L. R. Burleigh, Troy, New York	The Burleigh Lith. Est., Troy, New York	15×23½
635	Skaneateles 1884	L. R. Burleigh, Troy, New York	L. R. Burleigh, Troy, New York	Beck & Pauli, Litho., Milwaukee, Wisconsin	16×29½

No.	City and Date	Artist	Publisher	Lithographer or Printer	Map Size (Inches)
636	Stamford 1890		L. R. Burleigh, Troy, New York	Burleigh Lith. Est., Troy, New York	17×26
637	Stillwater 1889	L. R. Burleigh, Troy, New York	L. R. Burleigh, Troy, New York	The Burleigh Lith. Est., Troy, New York	17×26½
638	Syracuse 1868	J. C. Laass & L. Laass	E. Sachse & Co., Baltimore, Maryland	E. Sachse & Co., Baltimore, Maryland	In 2 parts, each 28½×78
639	Ticonderoga 1884	L. R. Burleigh, Troy, New York	L. R. Burleigh, Troy, New York	Beck & Pauli, Litho., Milwaukee, Wisconsin	18×24½
640	Ticonderoga 1891		R. M. Adkins, Ticonderoga, New York	Burleigh Lith. Est., Troy, New York	18½×25
641	Troy 1881			Beck & Pauli, Milwaukee, Wisconsin	29×36½
642	Unadilla 1887	L. R. Burleigh, Troy, New York	L. R. Burleigh, Troy, New York	The Burleigh Lith. Est., Troy, New York	14×25
643	Utica 1873	H. Brosius			25×33
644	Valley Falls 1887	L. R. Burleigh, Troy, New York	L. R. Burleigh, Troy, New York	Burleigh Lith. Est., Troy, New York	12×20
645	Valley Stream 1924	Rene Cinquin	Hughes & Cinquin, Brooklyn, New York	[Meriden Gravure Co., Meriden, Conn.]	22×34½
646	Walden 1887	L. R. Burleigh, Troy, New York	L. R. Burleigh, Troy, New York	The Burleigh Lith. Est., Troy, New York	15×24½
647	Walton 1887	L. R. Burleigh, Troy, New York	L. R. Burleigh, Troy, New York	Burleigh Lith. Est., Troy, New York	15×24
648	Wappingers Falls 1889	L. R. Burleigh, Troy, New York	L. R. Burleigh, Troy, New York	The Burleigh Lith. Est., Troy, New York	18×28
649	Warrensburgh 1891		L. R. Burleigh, Troy, New York	Burleigh Lith. Est., Troy, New York	18×31
650	Warsaw 1885	L. R. Burleigh, Troy, New York	L. R. Burleigh, Troy, New York	Beck & Pauli, Litho., Milwaukee, Wisconsin	15×28
651	Warwick 1887	L. R. Burleigh, Troy, New York	L. R. Burleigh, Troy, New York	The Burleigh Lith. Est., Troy, New York	14×20½

No.	City and Date	Artist	Publisher	Lithographer or Printer	Map Size (Inches)
652	Watertown 1891		J. C. Kimball, Watertown, New York	Burleigh Litho. Co., Troy, New York	20×35½
653	Waverly 1881	John Moray	John Moray	Thomas Hunter, Lith., Philadelphia, Pennsylvania	19×23
654	Weedsport 1885	L. R. Burleigh, Troy, New York	L. R. Burleigh, Troy, New York	C. H. Vogt & Son, Cleveland	13×26½
655	White Plains 1887	L. R. Burleigh, Troy, New York	L. R. Burleigh, Troy, New York	The Burleigh Lith. Est., Troy, New York	16×28½
656	Windsor 1887	L. R. Burleigh, Troy, New York	L. R. Burleigh, Troy, New York	The Burleigh Lith. Est., Troy, New York	16×21
657	Yonkers 1899		Landis & Hughes, New York		In 2 parts, each 43½×30

North Carolina

No.	City and Date	Artist	Publisher	Lithographer or Printer	Map Size (Inches)
658	Asheville 1891		Ruger & Stoner, Madison, Wisconsin	Burleigh Lith. Est., Troy, New York	26×31
659	Asheville 1912	T. M. Fowler, Passaic, N.J.	T. M. Fowler, Passaic, N.J.	Charles Hart, Photo., New York	24×34
660	Black Mountain 1912	[T. M. Fowler]	Fowler & Browning, Asheville, North Carolina	[Manhattan Photo Engraving Co., New York, New York]	24×32
661	Durham 1891 (with inset of East Durham)		Ruger & Stoner, Madison, Wisconsin	Burleigh Lith. Est., Troy, New York	18×29½
662	Greensboro 1891		Ruger & Stoner, Madison, Wisconsin	Burleigh Lith. Est., Troy, New York	17½×29
663	Hendersonville 1913	[T. M. Fowler]	Fowler & Browning, Asheville, North Carolina	[Manhattan Photo Engraving Co., New York, New York]	21½×31½
664	[Hickory 1907–08]	[A. E. Downs] (T. M. Fowler Map Coll. 12)			Manuscript, 17¾×28½

No.	City and Date	Artist	Publisher	Lithographer or Printer	Map Size (Inches)
665	High Point 1913	T. M. Fowler (T. M. Fowler Map Coll. 13)	J. J. Farris, High Point, N.C.	Charles Hart Litho., N.Y.	19×28
666	Raleigh 1872	C. N. Drie, Raleigh, N.C.	C. N. Drie, Raleigh, N.C.		24×29
667	Rocky Mount 1907	T. M. Fowler, Morrisville, Pa. (T. M. Fowler Map Coll. 14)	T. M. Fowler, Morrisville, Pa.	Chas. Hart Photo-Lith., New York	22×28
668	South Rock Mount [1907]	T. M. Fowler, Morrisville, Pa. (T. M. Fowler Map Coll. 15)			13½×18
669	[Statesville 1907–08]	[A. E. Downs] (T. M. Fowler Map Coll. 16)			Manuscript, 16½×26¾
670	Wilson 1908	T. M. Fowler, Morrisville, Pa.	T. M. Fowler, Morrisville, Pa.		22½×31
671	Winston-Salem 1891		Ruger & Stoner, Madison, Wisconsin		21×34

North Dakota

No.	City and Date	Artist	Publisher	Lithographer or Printer	Map Size (Inches)
672	Bismarck 1883		J. J. Stoner, Madison, Wisconsin	Beck & Pauli, Lith., Milwaukee, Wisconsin	16×26
672A	Fargo 1880 (Inset of Fargo 1872)	T. M. Fowler	J. J. Stoner, Madison, Wis.	Beck & Pauli, Lith., Milwaukee, Wis.	Film negative, 7×13
673	Jamestown 1883		J. J. Stoner, Madison, Wisconsin	Beck & Pauli, Milwaukee, Wisconsin	17×25½
674	Mandan 1883		J. J. Stoner, Madison, Wisconsin	Beck & Pauli, Milwaukee, Wisconsin	13½×22

No.	City and Date	Artist	Publisher	Lithographer or Printer	Map Size (Inches)

Ohio

No.	City and Date	Artist	Publisher	Lithographer or Printer	Map Size (Inches)
675	Akron 1870	A. Ruger	Ruger & Stoner, Madison, Wisconsin	Chicago Lith. Co., Chicago	23×28½
676	Akron (Sixth Ward) 1882 [Formerly Middlebury]		Ruger & Stoner, Madison, Wisconsin	Beck & Pauli, Milwaukee, Wisconsin	13×17½
677	Akron 1882		Ruger & Stoner, Madison, Wisconsin	Beck & Pauli, Lith., Milwaukee, Wisconsin	23×29
678	Ashtabula Harbor 1896	T. M. Fowler, Morrisville, Pa.	T. M. Fowler & James B. Moyer		20×26½
679	Barnesville 1899	T. M. Fowler, Morrisville, Pa.	T. M. Fowler & James B. Moyer		16×25½
680	Bellaire 1882 (Inset Benwood, West Virginia)	H. Wellge	J. J. Stoner, Madison, Wisconsin	Beck & Pauli, Milwaukee, Wisconsin	15×25
681	Bellevue 1888		Burleigh & Norris, Troy, New York	The Burleigh Lith. Est., Troy, New York	18×28½
682	Bowling Green 1888		Burleigh & Norris, Troy, New York	Burleigh Lith. Est., Troy, New York	19×27
683	Cambridge 1899	T. M. Fowler, Morrisville, Pa. (T. M. Fowler Map Coll. 17)	T. M. Fowler & James B. Moyer		19×32
684	Canal Dover 1899	A. E. Downs, Boston, Mass. (T. M. Fowler Map Coll. 18)	T. M. Fowler & A. E. Downs		21×28½
685	Cincinnati 1900	J. L. Trout, Cincinnati, Ohio	J. L. Trout, Cincinnati, Ohio	The Henderson Lith. Co., Cincinnati, Ohio	31×46
686	Circleville 1876		J. J. Stoner, Madison, Wisconsin	Krebs Lithographing Co., Cincinnati	21×25

No.	City and Date	Artist	Publisher	Lithographer or Printer	Map Size (Inches)
687	Cleveland 1877	A. Ruger	J. J. Stoner, Madison, Wisconsin	Shober & Carqueville, Chicago	18×34
688	Cleveland 1883				Photographic print, 10½×15
689	Cleveland 1887	C. H. Vogt & Son, Cleveland	C. H. Vogt & Son, Cleveland		15×21
690	Conneaut 1896	T. M. Fowler, Morrisville, Pa. (T. M. Fowler Map Coll. 19)	T. M. Fowler & James B. Moyer		20×29
691	Dayton 1870	[Albert Ruger]		Merchant's Lith. Co., Chicago	22½×31½
692	Elyria 1868	A. Ruger		Chicago Lith. Co., Chicago	21×24½
693	Findlay 1889		Burleigh & Norris, Troy, New York	The Burleigh Lith. Est., Troy, New York	22×34½
694	Kent 1882		Ruger & Stoner, Madison, Wisconsin	Beck & Pauli, Lith., Milwaukee, Wisconsin	18×26
695	Jefferson 1901	T. M. Fowler, Morrisville, Pa.	T. M. Fowler & James B. Moyer		Manuscript, 14×22
696	Lakeside 1884		A. J. Hare, **Sandusky**, Ohio	Sinz & Fausel Lith., Cleveland, Ohio	20½×25
697	Lima 1892		**Smith** & Buckingham	Geo. S. Harris & Sons, Philadelphia	30×39½
698	Martin's Ferry 1899	T. M. Fowler, Morrisville, Pa. (T. M. Fowler Map Coll. 20)	T. M. Fowler & James B. Moyer		19×24
699	Massillon 1870		Ruger & Stoner, Madison, Wisconsin	Merchant's Lith. Co., Chicago, Illinois	21×24½
700	Mingo Junction 1899	T. M. Fowler, Morrisville, Pa.	T. M. Fowler & James B. Moyer		15×23½
701	Mount Vernon 1870		Ruger & Stoner, Madison, Wisconsin	Merchant's Lith. Co., Chicago, Illinois	22½×24½

No.	City and Date	Artist	Publisher	Lithographer or Printer	Map Size (Inches)
702	Niles 1882		Ruger & Stoner, Madison, Wisconsin	Beck & Pauli, Lith., Milwaukee, Wisconsin	16½×22½
703	Norwalk 1870		Ruger & Stoner, Madison, Wisconsin	Merchant's Lith. Co., Chicago	20×24½
704	Ravenna 1882	[Albert Ruger]			18½×21
705	Sandusky 1870	A. Ruger	Ruger & Stoner, Madison, Wisconsin	Chicago Lith. Co.	20¾×25½
706	Sandusky 1883		A. J. Hare, Sandusky, Ohio	W. J. Morgan & Co., Cleveland, Ohio	26½×39½
707	Sandusky 1898		The Alvord-Peters Co., Sandusky, Ohio	The Gugler Litho. Co., Milwaukee, Wisconsin	17×36½
708	Scio 1899	T. M. Fowler, Morrisville, Pa.	T. M. Fowler, Morrisville, Pa.	Wheeling News Publishing Co.	17×24½
709	Scio 1899 [2d edition, April 1899]	T. M. Fowler, Morrisville, Pa.	T. M. Fowler & James B. Moyer		16×24½
710	Toledo 1876	A. Ruger	J. J. Stoner, Madison, Wisconsin	Chas. Shober & Co., Chicago Lith. Co.	12×26
711	Toronto 1899	A. E. Downs, Boston, Mass. (T. M. Fowler Map Coll. 21)	A. E. Downs & James B. Moyer		22×33½
712	Warren 1870		Ruger & Stoner, Madison, Wisconsin	Merchant's Lith. Co., Chicago, Illinois	21×26½
713	Youngstown 1882	A. Ruger	Ruger & Stoner, Madison, Wisconsin	Beck & Pauli, Lith., Milwaukee, Wisconsin	20½×28½

Oklahoma

No.	City and Date	Artist	Publisher	Lithographer or Printer	Map Size (Inches)
713A	Ardmore 1891	T. M. Fowler, Morrisville, Pa.	T. M. Fowler & James B. Moyer		14×23½

No.	City and Date	Artist	Publisher	Lithographer or Printer	Map Size (Inches)
714	Bartlesville, 1917	T. M. Fowler (T. M. Fowler Map Coll. 22)	Fowler & Kelley, Passaic, N.J.		14×29
714A	Fort Reno 1891	T. M. Fowler, Morrisville, Pa.	T. M. Fowler & James B. Moyer	A. E. Downs, Lith., Boston	11½×23½
715	Lawton 1910	Joslyn; J. P. Hathaway			6½×13½
715A	Oklahoma City 1890	T. M. Fowler, Morrisville, Pa.	T. M. Fowler, Morrisville, Pa.	A. E. Downs, Lith., Boston	8×10 film print
716	Tulsa 1918	[T. M. Fowler] (T. M. Fowler Map Coll. 23)	Fowler & Kelly	[Meriden Gravure Co., Meriden, Conn.]	15½×35

Oregon

No.	City and Date	Artist	Publisher	Lithographer or Printer	Map Size (Inches)
717	Jacksonville & the Rogue River Valley 1883	Fred A. Walpole	Fred A. Walpole	Beck & Pauli, Lith., Milwaukee, Wisconsin	17×22
718	Oregon City [185?]	J. H. Richardson, N.Y.			6×7½
719	Oregon City 1858		Charman & Warner, Oregon City		Photostatic positive, 16×22
720	Pendleton 1884	H. Wellge	J. J. Stoner, Madison, Wisconsin	Beck & Pauli, Lith., Milwaukee, Wisconsin	14×22
721	Pendleton [189?]		East Oregonian Publishing Co., Pendleton, Oregon	Dakin Publishing Co., San Francisco	21×28
722	Portland 1879	E. S. Glover	E. S. Glover	A. L. Bancroft & Co., San Francisco, California	25×40½
723	Portland 1881		J. K. Gill & Co., Portland, Oregon	A. L. Bancroft & Co., San Francisco, California	27×43
724	Portland 1890		Clohessy & Strengele	Elliott Pub. Co., S. F.	32×46

No.	City and Date	Artist	Publisher	Lithographer or Printer	Map Size (Inches)
725	Salem 1876	E. S. Glover	F. A. Smith, Salem, Oregon	A. L. Bancroft & Co., San Francisco, California	21½×30
726	Salem 1905		E. Koppe & Ch. Fromm	Mutual L. & Lith. Co., Portland, Oregon	27×35
727	The Dalles 1884	H. Wellge	J. J. Stoner, Madison, Wisconsin	Beck & Pauli, Milwaukee, Wisconsin	14½×24½

Pennsylvania

No.	City and Date	Artist	Publisher	Lithographer or Printer	Map Size (Inches)
728	Alburtis & Lockridge 1893	T. M. Fowler, Morrisville, Pa.	T. M. Fowler & James B. Moyer		12×18
729	Allentown 1901		Landis & Alsop, Newark, New Jersey		35½×50
730	Allentown 1922	T. M. Fowler (T. M. Fowler Map Coll. 24)	Hughes & Fowler		Manuscript, 29×75½
731	Allentown 1922	[T. M. Fowler] (T. M. Fowler Map Coll. 25)	Hughes & Fowler		Proof Copy, 14×35
732	Apollo 1896	T. M. Fowler, Morrisville, Pa.	T. M. Fowler & James B. Moyer		19½×24
733	Archbald 1892	T. M. Fowler, Morrisville, Pa.	T. M. Fowler & James B. Moyer	A. E. Downs, Boston	18×26
734	Bangor 1918	[T. M. Fowler] (T. M. Fowler Map Coll. 27)	Hughes & Bailey, Boston and New York		23×32
735	Beaver 1900	T. M. Fowler, Morrisville, Pa.	T. M. Fowler & James B. Moyer		18×24½
736	Belle Vernon 1902	T. M. Fowler, Morrisville, Pa.	T. M. Fowler & James B. Moyer		14×24
737	Berlin 1905	T. M. Fowler, Morrisville, Pa. (T. M. Fowler Map Coll. 28)	T. M. Fowler, Morrisville, Pa.		16×26

No.	City and Date	Artist	Publisher	Lithographer or Printer	Map Size (Inches)
738	Birdsboro 1890	T. M. Fowler, Morrisville, Pa.	T. M. Fowler & James B. Moyer	A. E. Downs, Boston	18×24
739	Bradford 1895	T. M. Fowler, Morrisville, Pa.	T. M. Fowler & James B. Moyer		22×33
740	Brookville 1895	T. M. Fowler, Morrisville, Pa.	T. M. Fowler & James B. Moyer		20×27
741	Brownsville 1902	T. M. Fowler, Morrisville, Pa.	T. M. Fowler & James B. Moyer		14×27
742	Burnham & Yeagertown 1906	T. M. Fowler, Morrisville, Pa.	Fowler & Kelly, Morrisville, Pa.		18×20
743	Butler 1896	T. M. Fowler, Morrisville, Pa.	T. M. Fowler & James B. Moyer		20½×30
744	California 1902	T. M. Fowler, Morrisville, Pa. (T. M. Fowler Map Coll. 78)	T. M. Fowler & James B. Moyer		12½×19
745	Cambridgeboro 1895	T. M. Fowler, Morrisville, Pa. (T. M. Fowler Map Coll. 29)	T. M. Fowler & James B. Moyer		18½×28
746	Canonsburg 1897	T. M. Fowler, Morrisville, Pa. (T. M. Fowler Map Coll. 70)	T. M. Fowler & James B. Moyer		18×24½
747	Carbondale 1890	T. M. Fowler, Morrisville, Pa.	T. M. Fowler & James B. Moyer	A. E. Downs, Lith., Boston	21½×36
748	Carnegie 1897	T. M. Fowler, Morrisville, Pa. (T. M. Fowler Map Coll. 72)	T. M. Fowler & James B. Moyer		18×29
'49	Chambersburg 1894	T. M. Fowler, Morrisville, Pa.	T. M. Fowler & James B. Moyer		8×10, film negative

No.	City and Date	Artist	Publisher	Lithographer or Printer	Map Size (Inches)
750	Charleroi 1897	T. M. Fowler, Morrisville, Pa.	T. M. Fowler & James B. Moyer		17×24
751	Chester 1885	[T. M. Fowler] (T. M. Fowler Map Coll. 30)	O. H. Bailey & Co., Boston	O. H. Bailey & Co., Boston	25½×31
752	Clarion 1896	T. M. Fowler, Morrisville, Pa.	T. M. Fowler & James B. Moyer		16½×23½
753	Clearfield 1895	T. M. Fowler, Morrisville, Pa.	T. M. Fowler & James B. Moyer		17½×27
754	Collegeville 1894	T. M. Fowler, Morrisville, Pa. (T. M. Fowler Map Coll. 31)	T. M. Fowler & James B. Moyer		18×26
755	Columbia 1894 [Inset of East Columbia]	T. M. Fowler, Morrisville, Pa. (T. M. Fowler Map Coll. 32)	T. M. Fowler & James B. Moyer		20×27
756	Confluence 1905	T. M. Fowler, Morrisville, Pa. (T. M. Fowler Map Coll. 33)	T. M. Fowler, Morrisville, Pa.		15¼×20
757	Connellsville 1897	T. M. Fowler, Morrisville, Pa. (T. M. Fowler Map Coll. 73)	T. M. Fowler & James B. Moyer		20×30½
758	Corry 1870	[Albert Ruger]	Ruger & Stoner, Madison, Wisconsin	Chicago Lithographing Co., Chicago	23×26
759	Corry 1895	T. M. Fowler, Morrisville, Pa. (T. M. Fowler Map Coll. 74)	T. M. Fowler & James B. Moyer		19×30
760	Curwensville 1895	T. M. Fowler, Morrisville, Pa.	T. M. Fowler & James B. Moyer		17×26

No.	City and Date	Artist	Publisher	Lithographer or Printer	Map Size (Inches)
761	Dawson 1902	T. M. Fowler, Morrisville, Pa. (T. M. Fowler Map Coll. 34)	T. M. Fowler, Morrisville, Pa.		15¼×19
762	Downingtown 1893	T. M. Fowler, Morrisville, Pa.	James B. Moyer, Myerstown, Pennsylvania		19×26½
763	DuBois 1895	T. M. Fowler, Morrisville, Pa.	T. M. Fowler & James B. Moyer		18½×34
764	Dunbar 1900	T. M. Fowler, Morrisville, Pa.	T. M. Fowler & James B. Moyer		14½×23
765	Duncannon 1903	T. M. Fowler, Morrisville, Pa. (T. M. Fowler Map Coll. 35)	T. M. Fowler, Morrisville, Pa.		15×20
766	Duquesne 1897	T. M. Fowler, Morrisville, Pa.	T. M. Fowler & James B. Moyer		19×27
767	Easton, Pennsylvania & Phillipsburg, New Jersey 1900		Landis & Alsop, Newark, New Jersey		32×39½
768	Edinboro 1898			John J. O'Brien, Erie, Pennsylvania	11½×22
769	Edwardsville 1892	T. M. Fowler, Morrisville, Pa.	T. M. Fowler & James B. Moyer		17×24½
770	Elizabeth & West Elizabeth 1897	T. M. Fowler, Morrisville, Pa.	T. M. Fowler & James B. Moyer		17½×26½
771	Emlenton 1897	T. M. Fowler, Morrisville, Pa.	T. M. Fowler & James B. Moyer		16×19½
772	Erie 1870	[Albert Ruger]	Ruger & Stoner, Madison, Wisconsin	Chicago Lithographing Co., Chicago	22½×34
773	Erie 1909	Chas Lederle & Co., Erie, Pa.	Chas. Lederle & Co., Erie, Pa.		29×40½

No.	City and Date	Artist	Publisher	Lithographer or Printer	Map Size (Inches)
774	Evans City 1900	T. M. Fowler, Morrisville, Pa.	T. M. Fowler & James B. Moyer		15×22½
775	Everett 1905	Thaddeus M. Fowler	Thaddeus M. Fowler		23×24
776	Ford City 1896	T. M. Fowler, Morrisville, Pa.	T. M. Fowler & James B. Moyer		17½×23
777	Forest City 1889	T. M. Fowler, Morrisville, Pa.	T. M. Folwer & James B. Moyer	A. E. Downs, Lith., Boston	19×26½
778	Franklin 1901	T. M. Fowler, Morrisville, Pa.	T. M. Fowler & James B. Moyer		20×31½
779	Gallitzin 1901	T. M. Fowler, Morrisville, Pa.	T. M. Fowler & James B. Moyer		14½×24½
780	Gettysburg 1888	T. M. Fowler & A. E. Downs, Boston	T. M. Fowler & A. E. Downs, Boston	A. E. Downs, Lith.	25×36
781	Glassport 1902	T. M. Fowler, Morrisville, Pa.	T. M. Fowler & James B. Moyer		13×21½
782	Great Bend 1887	L. R. Burleigh, Troy, New York	L. R. Burleigh, Troy, New York	The Burleigh Lith. Est., Troy, New York	15×20½
783	Greensburg 1901	T. M. Fowler, Morrisville, Pa.	T. M. Folwer & James B. Moyer		19×31½
784	Grove City 1901	T. M. Fowler, Morrisville, Pa.	T. M. Fowler & James B. Moyer		14×22½
785	Hallstead 1887	L. R. Burleigh, Troy, New York	L. R. Burleigh, Troy, New York	The Burleigh Lith. Est., Troy, New York	15×19½
786	Hamburg 1889	T. M. Fowler, Morrisville, Pa.	T. M. Fowler & F. P. Henry		21×28
787	Harmony 1901	T. M. Fowler, Morrisville, Pa.	T. M. Fowler & James B. Moyer		11½×16½
788	Harrisburg 1855	J. T. Williams, York, Pennsylvania		E. Sachse, Baltimore, Maryland	22½×32½

No.	City and Date	Artist	Publisher	Lithographer or Printer	Map Size (Inches)
789	Homestead 1902	T. M. Fowler, Morrisville, Pa.	T. M. Fowler & James B. Moyer		19×28
790	Honesdale 1890	T. M. Fowler, Morrisville, Pa.	T. M. Fowler & James B. Moyer	A. E. Downs, Lith., Boston	19×34½
791	Hyndman 1906	[T. M. Fowler]	Fowler & Kelly, Morrisville, Pennsylvania		18×19½
792	Indiana 1900	T. M. Fowler, Morrisville, Pa.	T. M. Fowler & James B. Moyer		17½×29
793	Irwin 1897	T. M. Fowler, Morrisville, Pa.	T. M. Fowler & James B. Moyer		18×25
794	Jeannette 1897	T. M. Fowler, Morrisville, Pa.	T. M. Fowler & James B. Moyer		19×30
795	Kittanning 1896	T. M. Fowler, Morrisville, Pa.	T. M. Fowler & James B. Moyer		17×27
795A	Knox 1896	T. M. Fowler, Morrisville, Pa.	T. M. Fowler & James B. Moyer		16×20 photograph
796	Latrobe 1900	T. M. Fowler, Morrisville, Pa.	T. M. Fowler & James B. Moyer		19½×30½
797	Ligonier 1900	T. M. Fowler, Morrisville, Pa. (T. M. Fowler Map Coll. 36)	T. M. Fowler & James B. Moyer		16×22½
798	McDonald 1897	T. M. Fowler, Morrisville, Pa.	T. M. Fowler & James B. Moyer		16×23
799	McKeesport 1893	Otto Krebs' Sons & Co., Pittsburgh, Pa.; H. Morgenroth	Otto Krebs' Sons & Co., Pittsburgh, Pa.	Otto Krebs' Sons & Co., Pittsburgh, Pa.	16×31
800	McKee's Rocks 1901	T. M. Fowler, Morrisville, Pa.	T. M. Fowler & James B. Moyer		21×26
801	Macungie 1893	T. M. Fowler, Morrisville, Pa.	T. M. Fowler & James B. Moyer		14½×20½

No.	City and Date	Artist	Publisher	Lithographer or Printer	Map Size (Inches)
802	Manayunk, Wissahickon-Roxborough 1907	T. M. Fowler, Morrisville, Pa.	Fowler & Kelly, Morrisville, Pa.		19×29
803	Millersburg 1894	T. M. Fowler, Morrisville, Pa.	T. M. Fowler & James B. Moyer		15×21½
804	Miner's Mills & Mill Creek 1892	T. M. Fowler, Morrisville, Pa.	T. M. Fowler & James B. Moyer		17×22
805	Minersville 1889	T. M. Fowler, Morrisville, Pa.			20×26½
806	Monaca 1900	T. M. Fowler, Morrisville, Pa. (T. M. Fowler Map Coll. 60)	T. M. Fowler & James B. Moyer		18×21
807	Monongahela City 1902	T. M. Fowler	T. M. Fowler & James B. Moyer		16×28
808	Moosic 1892	T. M. Fowler, Morrisville, Pa. (T. M. Fowler Map Coll. 37)	T. M. Fowler, Morrisville, Pa.	A. E. Downs, Lith., Boston	16×22
809	Morrisville 1893	T. M. Fowler, Morrisville, Pa. (T. M. Fowler Map Coll. 58)	T. M. Fowler, Morrisville, Pa.		20×31½
810	Moscow 1891	T. M. Fowler, Morrisville, Pa. (T. M. Fowler Map Coll. 38)	T. M. Fowler, Morrisville, Pa.		15½×20½
811	Mount Union 1906	T. M. Fowler, Morrisville, Pa.	Fowler & Kelly, Morrisville, Pa.		20×23½
812	Mountville 1894	T. M. Fowler, Morrisville, Pa.	T. M. Fowler & James B. Moyer		12½×14½
813	New Brighton 1901	T. M. Fowler, Morrisville, Pa.	T. M. Fowler & James B. Moyer		18×29

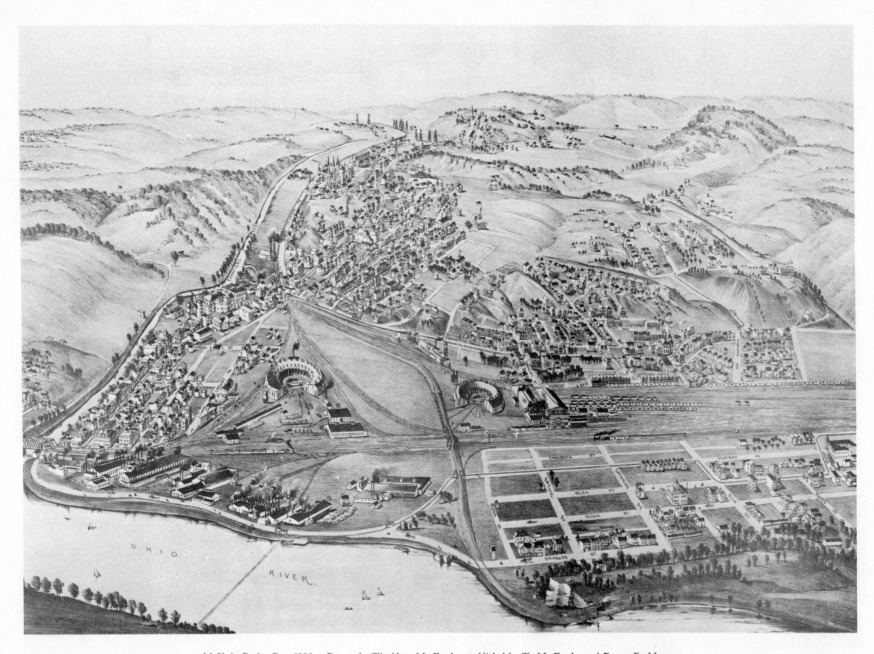

McKee's Rocks, Pa., 1901.   Drawn by Thaddeus M. Fowler; published by T. M. Fowler and James B. Moyer.

No.	City and Date	Artist	Publisher	Lithographer or Printer	Map Size (Inches)
814	New Castle 1896	T. M. Fowler, Morrisville, Pa. (T. M. Fowler Map Coll. 39)	T. M. Fowler & James B. Moyer		22×37½
815	New Kensington 1896	T. M. Fowler, Morrisville, Pa.	T. M. Fowler & James B. Moyer		19½×27½
816	New Kensington 1902	T. M. Fowler, Morrisville, Pa.	T. M. Fowler & James B. Moyer		14×20½
817	Newmanstown & Sheridan 1898	[T. M. Fowler]	Bailey & Moyer, Boston, Massachusetts		13×20
818	Newville 1903	T. M. Fowler, Morrisville, Pa. (T. M. Fowler Map Coll. 40)	T. M. Fowler, Morrisville, Pa.		15×20
819	Norristown 1881		Packard & Butler, Philadelphia		22×34
820	Northeast 1896	T. M. Fowler, Morrisville, Pa.	T. M. Fowler & James B. Moyer		20×28
821	Oil City 1896	T. M. Fowler, Morrisville, Pa.	T. M. Fowler & James B. Moyer		21½×32½
822	Orbisonia & Rock Hill 1906		Fowler & Kelly, Morrisville, Pa.		17×20½
823	Oxford 1907		Fowler & Kelly, Morrisville, Pa.		20×23
824	Peckville 1892	T. M. Fowler, Morrisville, Pa.	T. M. Fowler & James B. Moyer	A. E. Downs, Lith., Boston	18×25½
825	Pen Argyl 1894	T. M. Fowler, Morrisville, Pa.	T. M. Fowler & James B. Moyer		18×27
826	Pen Argyl 1916	T. M. Fowler, Morrisville, Pa. (T. M. Fowler Map Coll. 41)	Hughes & Bailey, New York	[Meriden Gravure Co., Meriden, Conn. & Tudor Press, Boston]	20×34½

No.	City and Date	Artist	Publisher	Lithographer or Printer	Map Size (Inches)
827	Philadelphia 1857	J. Bachman	John Weik, Philadelphia	P. S. Duval & Sons, Lith., Philadelphia	31×36
828	Philadelphia 1872	Theodore R. Davis	Harper & Brothers		21½×30
829	Philadelphia 1876				23×30
830	Philadelphia 1887			Burk & McFetridge, Philadelphia	20×34
831	Philadelphia 1888			Burk & McFetridge, Philadelphia	20×34
832	Pitcairn 1901	T. M. Fowler, Morrisville, Pa. (T. M. Fowler Map Coll. 42)	T. M. Fowler & James B. Moyer		13½×20
833	Pittsburgh 1902	T. M. Fowler, Morrisville, Pa.	T. M. Fowler & James B. Moyer		15×23
834	Point Marion 1902	T. M. Fowler, Morrisville, Pa.	T. M. Fowler, Morrisville, Pa.		15×20½
835	Pottsville 1889	T. M. Fowler, Morrisville, Pa.	T. M. Fowler & James B. Moyer	A. E. Downs, Lith., Boston	20×34½
836	Providence 1892	A. E. Downs, Boston (T. M. Fowler Map Coll. 43)			Manuscript, 22×35
837	Reading 1881	J. Hanold Kendall			25×32
838	Ridgway 1895	T. M. Fowler, **Morrisville, Pa.**	T. M. Fowler & James B. Moyer		19×29½
839	Rochester 1900	**T. M. Fowler, Morrisville, Pa.**	T. M. Fowler & James B. Moyer		19×30½
840	Roscoe 1902	T. M. Fowler, Morrisville, Pa.	T. M. Fowler & James B. Moyer		12×19
841	St. Mary's 1895	T. M. Fowler, Morrisville, Pa.	T. M. Fowler & James B. Moyer		19×26

No.	City and Date	Artist	Publisher	Lithographer or Printer	Map Size (Inches)
842	Schwenksville 1894	T. M. Fowler	T. M. Fowler & James B. Moyer		15×21
843	Scottdale & Everson 1890		[Scottdale & Everson Land Co.]		6×9
844	Scranton 1890	T. M. Fowler & A. E. Downs	T. M. Fowler & James B. Moyer	A. E. Downs, Lith., Boston	24×40½
845	Sellersville 1894	T. M. Fowler, Morrisville, Pa.	T. M. Fowler & James B. Moyer		16×25
846	Sharon 1901	T. M. Fowler, Morrisville, Pa.	T. M. Fowler & James B. Moyer		18½×30½
847	Sharpsville 1901	T. M. Fowler, Morrisville, Pa.	T. M. Fowler & James B. Moyer		15×24
848	Sheffield 1895	T. M. Fowler, Morrisville, Pa.	T. M. Fowler & James B. Moyer		17×25
849	Shenandoah 1889	T. M. Fowler, Morrisville, Pa.	T. M. Fowler & J. B. Moyer		21×29
850	Shippensburg 1894	T. M. Fowler, Morrisville, Pa.	T. M. Fowler & James B. Moyer		8×10, film negative
851	Somerset 1900	T. M. Fowler, Morrisville, Pa.	T. M. Fowler & James B. Moyer		19½×24
852	Souderton 1894	T. M. Fowler, Morrisville, Pa.	T. M. Fowler & James B. Moyer		16×20
853	South Fork 1900	T. M. Fowler, Morrisville, Pa.	T. M. Fowler & James B. Moyer		16×23
854	Strasburg 1903	T. M. Fowler, Morrisville, Pa. (T. M. Fowler Map Coll. 44)	T. M. Fowler, Morrisville, Pa.		13×18
855	Tarentum 1901	T. M. Fowler, Morrisville, Pa.	T. M. Fowler & James B. Moyer		17×29½

No.	City and Date	Artist	Publisher	Lithographer or Printer	Map Size (Inches)
856	Telford 1894	T. M. Fowler, Morrisville, Pa. (T. M. Fowler Map Coll. 61)	T. M. Fowler & James B. Moyer		14×20
857	Terre Hill 1894	T. M. Fowler, Morrisville, Pa. (T. M. Fowler Map Coll. 45)	T. M. Fowler & James B. Moyer		15½×21½
858	Tidioute 1896	T. M. Fowler, Morrisville, Pa. (T. M. Fowler Map Coll. 46)	T. M. Fowler & James B. Moyer		17×24½
859	Tionesta 1896	T. M. Fowler, Morrisville, Pa. (T. M. Fowler Map Coll. 47)	T. M. Fowler & James B. Moyer		13½×18
860	Titusville 1871	A. Ruger		Chicago Lithographing Co., Chicago	23×26½
861	Titusville 1896	T. M. Fowler, Morrisville, Pa.	T. M. Fowler & James B. Moyer		21×34
862	Topton 1893	T. M. Fowler, Morrisville, Pa. (T. M. Fowler Map Coll. 48)	T. M. Fowler & James B. Moyer		13×20
863	Tullytown 1887	T. M. Fowler (T. M. Fowler Map Coll. 49)			12×17½
864	Turtle Creek 1897	T. M. Fowler, Morrisville, Pa. (T. M. Fowler Map Coll. 50)	T. M. Fowler & James B. Moyer		16×22½
864A	Tyrone 1895	T. M. Fowler, Morrisville, Pa. (T. M. Fowler Map Coll. 68)	T. M. Fowler & James B. Moyer		14½×24½
865	Union City 1895	T. M. Fowler, Morrisville, Pa.	T. M. Fowler & James B. Moyer		19×26½

No.	City and Date	Artist	Publisher	Lithographer or Printer	Map Size (Inches)
866	Uniontown 1897	T. M. Fowler, Morrisville, Pa.	T. M. Fowler & James B. Moyer		20½×27
867	Valley Forge 1890	[T. M. Fowler] (T. M. Fowler Map Coll. 51)	James B. Moyer, Myerstown, Pa.	A. E. Downs, Lith., Boston	19×26
868	Verona & Oakmont 1896	T. M. Fowler, Morrisville, Pa.	T. M. Fowler & James B. Moyer		20×28½
869	Washington 1897	T. M. Fowler, Morrisville, Pa.	T. M. Fowler & James B. Moyer		21×38
870	Waynesburg 1897	T. M. Fowler, Morrisville, Pa.	T. M. Fowler & James B. Moyer		17½×23
871	West Newton 1900	T. M. Fowler, Morrisville, Pa.	T. M. Fowler & James B. Moyer		17×24
872	Wilkes-Barre 1889	Fowler, Downs & Moyer	Fowler, Downs & Moyer	A. E. Downs, Lith., Boston	26×42½
873	Williamsburg 1906	T. M. Fowler, Morrisville, Pa.	Fowler & Kelly, Morrisville, Pa.		22×24½
874	Wilmerding 1897	T. M. Fowler, Morrisville, Pa.	T. M. Fowler & James B. Moyer		17½×23½
875	Wilson & Mendelssohn 1902	T. M. Fowler, Morrisville, Pa.	T. M. Fowler & James B. Moyer		10×13
875A	Windber 1900 (with Scalp Level)	T. M. Fowler, Morrisville, Pa.	T. M. Fowler & James B. Moyer		16×20 photograph
876	Wrightsville 1894	T. M. Fowler, Morrisville, Pa.	T. M. Fowler & James B. Moyer		16×22
876A	York 1852		J. Thomas Williams	E. Sachse & Co., Baltimore	19×27
877	York 1879	Davoust Kern	Davoust Kern	A. Hoen & Co., Lith., Baltimore, Maryland	24×37½
878	Zelienople 1901	T. M. Fowler, Morrisville, Pa.	T. M. Fowler & James B. Moyer		14×21½

No.	City and Date	Artist	Publisher	Lithographer or Printer	Map Size (Inches)
Rhode Island					
879	Newport 1878	Galt & Hoy, New York	Galt & Hoy, New York		25×27½
879A	Pascoag 1895		O. H. Bailey & Co.	O. H. Bailey & Co.	8×10 photograph
880	Pawtucket & Central Falls 1877	O. H. Bailey & J. C. Hazen, Boston	O. H. Bailey & J. C. Hazen, Boston	C. H. Vogt, Lith., Milwaukee; J. Knauber & Co.	25×32½
881	Providence 1896	M. D. Mason			16×20
882	Westerly 1911		Hughes & Bailey, New York		29½×36
South Carolina					
883	Charleston 1872	C. Drie	C. Drie	C. Drie	22½×33½
884	Columbia 1872	C. Drie	C. Drie		22½×28
South Dakota					
885	Aberdeen 1883	H. Wellge	F. H. Hagerty & H. M. Marple, Aberdeen, Dakota Territory		15×25
886	Clark 1883		J. J. Stoner, Madison, Wisconsin	Beck & Pauli, Lith., Milwaukee, Wisconsin	12×18
887	Deadwood 1884	W. V. Herancourt	Reproduced in 1969 by Historic Urban Plans, Ithaca, New York		13×20½
888	Flandreau 1883	H. Brosius	J. J. Stoner, Madison, Wisconsin	Beck & Pauli, Milwaukee, Wisconsin	13×21
889	Frederick 1883		C. F. Campau		12×16

No.	City and Date	Artist	Publisher	Lithographer or Printer	Map Size (Inches)
890	Madison 1883	H. Brosius	J. J. Stoner, Madison, Wisconsin	Beck & Pauli, Milwaukee, Wisconsin	13×20
891	Redfield 1883	H. Wellge	The Dakota Sun & Job Printing House, H. G. Rising, prop.		12×15½
892	Watertown 1883		J. J. Stoner, Madison, Wisconsin	Beck & Pauli, Milwaukee, Wisconsin	13½×21

Tennessee

No.	City and Date	Artist	Publisher	Lithographer or Printer	Map Size (Inches)
893	Chattanooga 1871	A. Ruger, St. Louis, Mo.	A. Ruger, St. Louis, Mo.		23×31
894	Chattanooga 1886	H. Wellge	Norris, Wellge & Co., Milwaukee, Wisconsin	Beck & Pauli, Lith., Milwaukee, Wisconsin	21×28½
895	Chattanooga 1887				20×25
896	Clarksville 1870	[Albert Ruger]	Stoner & Ruger	Merchant Lith. Co., Chicago	23×26
897	Harriman 1892	Geo. E. Norris, Brockton, Mass.	Geo. E. Norris, Brockton, Mass.	The Burleigh Lith. Co., Troy, New York	21×29½
898	Jackson 1870	A. Ruger		Chicago Litho. Co., Chicago, Illinois	22½×26½
899	Knoxville 1871	[Albert Ruger]		Merchants Lith. Co., Chicago	23×26½
900	Knoxville 1886	H. Wellge	Norris, Wellge & Co., Milwaukee, Wisconsin	Beck & Pauli, Litho., Milwaukee, Wisconsin	21×28½
901	Memphis 1870	[Albert Ruger]			20×33¾
902	Memphis 1887		Henry Wellge & Co., Milwaukee, Wisconsin		28×41

Texas

No.	City and Date	Artist	Publisher	Lithographer or Printer	Map Size (Inches)
903	Amarillo (Business District) 1912	E. E. Motter	G. C. Sturdivant	Panhandle Printing Co., Amarillo	17×19½

No.	City and Date	Artist	Publisher	Lithographer or Printer	Map Size (Inches)
904	Brenham 1881	Augustus Koch			8×10, film negative
905	Childress 1890	T. M. Fowler, Morrisville, Pa. (T. M. Fowler Map Coll. 52)	T. M. Fowler & James B. Moyer		10×16½
906	Clarendon 1890	T. M. Fowler, Morrisville, Pa. (T. M. Fowler Map Coll. 53)	T. M. Fowler & James B. Moyer		14½×25
907	Dallas 1892	Paul Giraud	Paul Giraud	Dallas Lith. Co.	21×29
908	Denison 1886		Norris, Wellge & Co., Milwaukee, Wisconsin	Beck & Pauli, Lith., Milwaukee, Wisconsin	20×27
908A	Denison 1891	T. M. Fowler, Morrisville, Pa.	T. M. Fowler & James B. Moyer		21×33½
909	Fort Griffin 184?				Photostatic negative, 11×20
910	Fort Worth 1886	H. Wellge	Norris, Wellge & Co., Milwaukee, Wisconsin	Beck & Pauli, Litho., Milwaukee, Wisconsin	26½×34
911	Fort Worth 1891	H. Wellge	American Publishing Co., Milwaukee, Wisconsin		20×33½
912	Fort Worth 1913	A. S. Harris			Film print, 4×9½
913	Greenville 1886	H. Wellge	Norris, Wellge & Co., Milwaukee, Wisconsin	Beck & Pauli, Lith., Milwaukee, Wisconsin	18×25
914	Honey Grove 1886	H. Wellge	Norris, Wellge & Co., Milwaukee, Wisconsin	Beck & Pauli, Lith., Milwaukee, Wisconsin	17×21½
915	Houston 1891	[A. L. Westyard]	D. W. Ensign, Jr., Chicago		28×43
916	Houston 1912	Hopkins & Motter	Hopkins & Motter		16½×21

No.	City and Date	Artist	Publisher	Lithographer or Printer	Map Size (Inches)
917	Jefferson 1872	H. Brosius	Reproduced in 1937 by A. Paul Brooks, United Gas Corporation		20×27½
918	Laredo 1892	[H. Wellge]	American Publishing Co., Milwaukee, Wisconsin		22½×33½
919	Paris 1885	[H. Wellge]	Norris, Wellge & Co., Milwaukee, Wisconsin	Beck & Pauli, Milwaukee, Wisconsin	19½×25½
920	Port Arthur 1912	E. S. Glover	Port Arthur Board of Trade		16×36½
920A	Quanah 1890	T. M. Fowler, Morrisville, Pa.	T. M. Fowler & James B. Moyer		11×14 photograph
921	Waco 1886	[H. Wellge]	Norris, Wellge & Co., Milwaukee, Wisconsin	Beck & Pauli, Milwaukee, Wisconsin	22½×31
922	Waco 1892	A. L. Westyard	D. W. Ensign & Co.	Shober & Carqueville Lith., Chicago	43×25
922A	Wolfe City 1891	T. M. Fowler, Morrisville, Pa.	T. M. Fowler & James B. Moyer		15×21

Utah

No.	City and Date	Artist	Publisher	Lithographer or Printer	Map Size (Inches)
923	Brigham City & Great Salt Lake 1875	E. S. Glover, Salt Lake City	E. S. Glover, Salt Lake City	Strobridge & Co., Cincinnati, Ohio	16×22½
924	Ogden 1875	E. S. Glover	E. S. Glover	Strobridge & Co., Cincinnati, Ohio	17×22½
925	Ogden 1889	Eugene F. Darling	Eugene F. Darling		22×37
926	Ogden 1890	[H. Wellge]	American Publishing Co., Milwaukee, Wisconsin		20×35½
927	Salt Lake City 1867		Philip Ritz, Walla Walla, W. T. Reproduced in 1969 by Historic Urban Plans, Ithaca, New York	H. J. Toudy, Phila	14×26

No.	City and Date	Artist	Publisher	Lithographer or Printer	Map Size (Inches)
928	Salt Lake City 1870	Augustus Koch	Augustus Koch	Chicago Litho. Co.	29×35
929	Salt Lake City 1875	E. S. Glover	E. S. Glover	Strobridge & Co., Cincinnati, Ohio	24½×32½
930	Salt Lake City 1891	H. Wellge	American Publishing Co., Milwaukee, Wisconsin		24×44½

Vermont

No.	City and Date	Artist	Publisher	Lithographer or Printer	Map Size (Inches)
931	Barre 1891	Geo. E. Norris, Brockton, Mass.	Geo. E. Norris, Brockton, Mass.		19×30½
932	Bellows Falls 1886		L. R. Burleigh	The Burleigh Lith. Est., Troy, New York	17×26½
933	Bennington 1887	L. R. Burleigh	L. R. Burleigh	Burleigh Litho., Troy, New York	19×31½
934	Bethel 1886		L. R. Burleigh, Troy, New York	The Burleigh Lith. Est., Troy, New York	14×21
935	Brattleboro 1886	L. R. Burleigh		The Burleigh Lith. Est., Troy, New York	14×27½
936	Bristol 1889 (with Rockydale)	Geo. E. Norris, Brockton, Mass.	Geo. E. Norris, Brockton, Mass.	The Burleigh Lith. Est., Troy, New York	16×26½
937	Fairhaven 1886	L. R. Burleigh, Troy, New York	L. R. Burleigh, Troy, New York		13×23½
938	Hardwick 1892 (with Granite Junction)		Geo. E. Norris, Brockton, Massachusetts		17×21½
939	Ludlow 1885	L. R. Burleigh, Troy, New York	L. R. Burleigh, Troy, New York		16×23½
940	Middlebury 1886	L. R. Burleigh, Troy, New York	L. R. Burleigh, Troy, New York	Beck & Pauli, Litho., Milwaukee, Wisconsin	14×25
941	Morrisville 1889	Geo. E. Norris, Brockton, Mass.	Geo. E. Norris, Brockton, Mass.	The Burleigh Lith. Est., Troy, New York	14½×21½

No.	City and Date	Artist	Publisher	Lithographer or Printer	Map Size (Inches)
942	Poultney 1886	L. R. Burleigh, Troy, New York	L. R. Burleigh, Troy, New York	C. H. Vogt & Son, Lith., Cleveland, Ohio	14×20½
943	Rutland 1885	L. R. Burleigh, Troy, New York	L. R. Burleigh, Troy, New York	C. H. Vogt & Son, Lith., Cleveland, Ohio	18×31
944	St. Johnsbury 1884	H. W. Studley & Geo. E. Norris	Geo. E. Norris, Brockton, Massachusetts	Beck & Pauli, Litho., Milwaukee, Wisconsin	22×32½
945	Springfield 1886	L. R. Burleigh, Troy, New York	L. R. Burleigh, Troy, New York	Beck & Pauli, Milwaukee, Wisconsin	14×25½
946	Vergennes 1890			The Burleigh Lith. Est., Troy, New York	20×29
947	West Randolph 1886		L. R. Burleigh	The Burleigh Lith. Est., Troy, New York	16×24
948	Wilmington 1891		L. R. Burleigh	Burleigh Lith. Est., Troy, New York	15½×25½
949	Windsor 1886	L. R. Burleigh, Troy, New York	L. R. Burleigh, Troy, New York	Burleigh Lith. Est., Troy, New York	15×23½

Virginia

No.	City and Date	Artist	Publisher	Lithographer or Printer	Map Size (Inches)
950	Alexandria 1863	[Charles Magnus]	Chas. Magnus, Washington, D.C.		16×23
951	Bedford City 1891	H. Wellge	American Publishing Co., Milwaukee, Wisconsin		20×29
952	Bristol, Virginia-Tennessee 1912	T. M. Fowler, Passaic, N.J.	T. M. Fowler, Passaic, N.J.	[Charles Hart, New York, New York]	29×34½
953	Buena Vista 1891	[H. Wellge]	American Publishing Co., Milwaukee, Wisconsin		21×33½
954	Emporia 1907	T. M. Fowler, Morrisville, Pa.	T. M. Fowler, Morrisville, Pa.		24×28
955	Franklin 1907	T. M. Fowler, Morrisville, Pa.	T. M. Fowler, Morrisville, Pa.		18½×24

No.	City and Date	Artist	Publisher	Lithographer or Printer	Map Size (Inches)
956	Fredericksburg 1862		E. Sachse & Co., Baltimore	E. Sachse & Co., Baltimore	10½×17 (In Civil War Bibliography 554)
957	Newport News	[H. Wellge]	American Publishing Co., Milwaukee, Wisconsin		22×34
958	Norfolk & Portsmouth 1873	C. N. Drie	C. N. Drie		23×34
959	Norfolk, Portsmouth, & Berkley 1891	Augustus Koch	Augustus Koch	Morning News Lith., Savannah, Ga.	31½×41
960	Norfolk & Surroundings 1892	H. Wellge	American Publishing Co., Milwaukee, Wisconsin; Hume & Bilisoly, Pub. Agt's, Norfolk		24×40½
961	Pocahontas 1911	T. M. Fowler, Flemington, N.J. (T. M. Fowler Map Coll. 54)	T. M. Fowler, Flemington, N.J.		16½×25¼
962	Roanoke 1891	[H. Wellge]	American Publishing Co., Milwaukee, Wisconsin		23½×39
963	Staunton 1891	[H. Wellge]	American Publishing Co., Milwaukee, Wisconsin		21½×32½
964	Suffolk 1907	T. M. Fowler, Morrisville, Pa.	Fowler & Kelly, Morrisville, Pa.		24×35½
965	Waynesboro 1891	[H. Wellge]	American Publishing Co., Milwaukee, Wisconsin		22×32½
966	Winchester 1926	Woods	W. A. Ryan		15×20

Washington

No.	City and Date	Artist	Publisher	Lithographer or Printer	Map Size (Inches)
967	Cheney 1884	H. Wellge	J. J. Stoner, Madison, Wisconsin	Beck & Pauli, Lith., Milwaukee, Wisconsin	14×20

No.	City and Date	Artist	Publisher	Lithographer or Printer	Map Size (Inches)
968	Dayton 1884	H. Wellge	J. J. Stoner, Madison, Wisconsin	Beck & Pauli, Lith., Milwaukee, Wisconsin	15×25
969	North Yakima 1889	The Spike & Arnold Map Publishing Co.; W. Arnold	The Spike & Arnold Map Publishing Co.		24×31½
970	Olympia, East Olympia & Tumwater 1879	E. S. Glover, Portland, Oregon	E. S. Glover, Portland, Oregon	A. L. Bancroft & Co., San Francisco	20×30
971	Olympia 1903	Edw. Lange, Olympia, Wash.	Edw. Lange, Olympia, Wash.	Franklin Engraving & Electrotyping Co., Chicago, Illinois	17½×20½
972	Port Townsend 1878	E. S. Glover, Portland, Oregon	E. S. Glover, Portland, Oregon	A. L. Bancroft, San Francisco, California	17×25
973	Seattle 1878	E. S. Glover, Portland	E. S. Glover, Portland	A. L. Bancroft & Co., San Francisco	19½×30½
974	Seattle 1884	H. Wellge	J. J. Stoner, Madison, Wisconsin	Beck & Pauli, Lith., Milwaukee, Wisconsin	17×32½
975	Seattle & Environs 1891	Augustus Koch	Augustus Koch	Hughes Litho. Co., Chicago	34×50½
976	Seattle (Main Businesss District) 1903	Ross M. Tulloch	Periscopic Map Co., W. P. C. Adams, Mgr.		20×21
977	Seattle 1925	Edwin C. Poland	Kroll Map Co.		32×55½
978	Spokane 1905 (Inset of Fort Wright)		John W. Graham & Co., Spokane, Wash.		39×60
979	Tacoma, New Tacoma & Mount Rainier 1878	E. S. Glover, Portland	E. S. Glover, Portland	A. L. Bancroft & Co., San Francisco	17×25
980	Tacoma 1884	H. Wellge	J. J. Stoner, Madison, Wisconsin	Beck & Pauli, Lith., Milwaukee, Wisconsin	16×33
981	Tacoma 1885				17×34

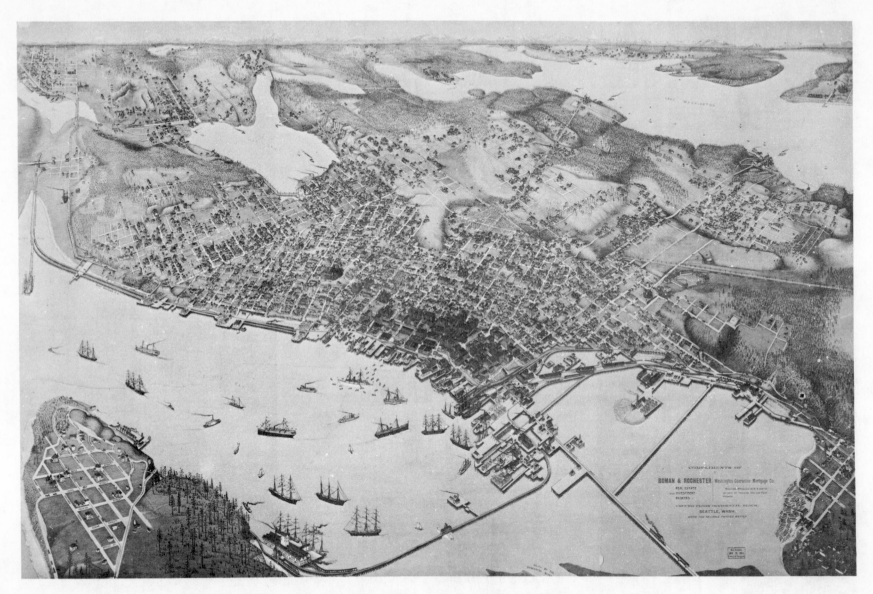

Seattle, Wash., and environs, 1891, "Eighteen months after the great fire."   Drawn by Augustus Koch.

96

No.	City and Date	Artist	Publisher	Lithographer or Printer	Map Size (Inches)
982	Tacoma 1890	Will Carson			32×43½
982A	Tacoma 1890		Geo. W. Traver [Tacoma]		Photostat in 2 parts, 19×16 ea.
983	Walla Walla 1876	E. S. Glover	Everts & Able, Walla Walla	A. L. Bancroft & Co., San Francisco	19×28½
984	Walla Walla 1884 (On verso Fairport, New York, by Burleigh 1885)	H. Wellge	J. J. Stoner, Madison, Wisconsin	Beck & Pauli, Lith., Milwaukee, Wisconsin	18×27½

West Virginia

No.	City and Date	Artist	Publisher	Lithographer or Printer	Map Size (Inches)
985	Bayard 1898	T. M. Fowler, Morrisville, Pa.	T. M. Fowler, Morrisville, Pa.		14×17
986	Berkeley Springs 1889		John Moray	A. Hoen & Co., Lith. Baltimore, Maryland	20×23½
987	Bluefield 1911	T. M. Fowler (T. M. Fowler Map Coll. 55)	Fowler & Basham, Flemington, New Jersey		18½×38½
988	Buckhannon 1900	T. M. Fowler, Morrisville, Pa.	T. M. Fowler & James B. Moyer		15×23½
989	Cairo 1899	T. M. Fowler, Morrisville, Pa. (T. M. Fowler Map Coll. 76)	T. M. Fowler & James B. Moyer		18×22½
990	Cameron 1899	T. M. Fowler, Morrisville, Pa. (T. M. Fowler Map Coll. 64)	T. M. Fowler, Morrisville, Pa.	Wheeling News Lith., Wheeling, West Virginia	17½×22½
991	Clarksburg 1898	T. M. Fowler, Morrisville, Pa. (T. M. Fowler Map Coll. 71)	T. M. Fowler & James B. Moyer		20½×28

No.	City and Date	Artist	Publisher	Lithographer or Printer	Map Size (Inches)
992	Davis 1898	T. M. Fowler, Morrisville, Pa.	T. M. Fowler, Morrisville, Pa.		17×24
993	Elkins 1897	T. M. Fowler, Morrisville, Pa.	T. M. Fowler & James B. Moyer		18×24½
994	Fairmont & Palatine 1897	T. M. Fowler, Morrisville, Pa. (T. M. Fowler Map Coll. 77)	T. M. Fowler & James B. Moyer		20½×29
995	Grafton 1898	A. E. Downs, Boston, Mass.	Fowler & Downs, Boston, Mass.		23×26½
996	Harrisville 1899	T. M. Fowler, Morrisville, Pa.	T. M. Fowler & James B. Moyer		13×20
997	Keyser 1905	T. M. Fowler, Morrisville, Pa.	Fowler & Kelly		8×10 Photograph Negative
998	Keystone 1911	[T. M. Fowler] (T. M. Fowler Map Coll. 56)	T. M. Fowler, Flemington, New Jersey		9½×20
999	Mannington 1897	T. M. Fowler, Morrisville, Pa.	T. M. Fowler & James B. Moyer		17½×22½
1000	Morgantown 1897	T. M. Fowler, Morrisville, Pa.	T. M. Fowler & James B. Moyer		19×28
1001	Moundsville 1899	A. E. Downs, Boston, Mass. (T. M. Fowler Map Coll. 75)	James B. Moyer, Myerstown, Pennsylvania		20×25½
1002	New Martinsville 1899	T. M. Fowler, Morrisville, Pa.	T. M. Fowler & James B. Moyer		18½×24½
1003	North Fork and Clark 1911	[T. M. Fowler] (T. M. Fowler Map Coll. 57)	T. M. Fowler, Flemington, New Jersey		9×18
1004	Parkersburg [1861]			A. Hoen & Co., Baltimore	20×31

Philippi, W. Va., 1897.   Drawn by Thaddeus M. Fowler; published by Thaddeus M. Fowler and James B. Moyer.

No.	City and Date	Artist	Publisher	Lithographer or Printer	Map Size (Inches)
1005	Parkersburg 1899	T. M. Fowler, Morrisville, Pa.	T. M. Fowler & James B. Moyer		20×32½
1006	Parsons 1905	Fowler & Kelly, Morrisville, Pa.	Fowler & Kelly, Morrisville, Pa.		20×22
1007	Pennsboro 1899	T. M. Fowler, Morrisville, Pa. (T. M. Fowler Map Coll. 63)	T. M. Fowler & James B. Moyer		14×20½
1008	Philippi 1861	Mrs. M. D. Pool, Virginia			21×30
1009	Philippi 1897	T. M. Fowler, Morrisville, Pa.	T. M. Fowler & James B. Moyer		12×15½
1010	St. Mary's 1899	T. M. Fowler, Morrisville, Pa.	T. M. Fowler & James B. Moyer		12½×20½
1011	Salem 1899	T. M. Fowler, Morrisville, Pa.	T. M. Fowler & James B. Moyer		15×23
1012	Sistersville 1896	T. M. Fowler, Morrisville, Pa. (T. M. Fowler Map Coll. 67)	T. M. Fowler & James B. Moyer		16×21½
1013	Wellsburg 1899	T. M. Fowler, Morrisville, Pa.	T. M. Fowler, Morrisville, Pa.		8×10 Photograph Negative
1014	Weston 1900	T. M. Fowler, Morrisville, Pa.	T. M. Fowler & James B. Moyer		14×23½
1015	West Union 1899	T. M. Fowler, Morrisville, Pa.	T. M. Fowler & James B. Moyer		8×10 Photograph Negative
1016	Wheeling 1870	[Albert Ruger]	Ruger & Stoner, Madison, Wisconsin	Chicago Lithographing Co., Chicago, Illinois	22½×34

Wisconsin

No.	City and Date	Artist	Publisher	Lithographer or Printer	Map Size (Inches)
1017	Antigo 1885		Norris, Wellge & Co., Milwaukee, Wisconsin	Beck & Pauli, Lith., Milwaukee, Wisconsin	17×23

No.	City and Date	Artist	Publisher	Lithographer or Printer	Map Size (Inches)
1018	Appleton 1867	A. Ruger, Chicago		Chicago Lith. Co.	22×28
1019	Ashland 1886	H. Welg [H. Wellge]	Norris, Wellge & Co., Milwaukee, Wisconsin	Beck & Pauli, Lith., Milwaukee, Wisconsin	20×35½
1020	Ashland, Lake Superior 1890	C. J. Pauli, Milwaukee, Wis.	The Ashland Daily Press	Marr & Richards Engraving, Milwaukee	23×41
1021	Bayfield 1886	H. Wellge	Norris, Wellge & Co., Milwaukee, Wisconsin	Beck & Pauli, Lith., Milwaukee, Wisconsin	17×20½
1022	Beaver Dam 1867	A. Ruger		Chicago Lith. Co.	22½×24½
1023	Beloit 1890	[H. Wellge]	American Publishing Co., Milwaukee, Wisconsin		22½×28
1024	Berlin 1867	A. Ruger		Chicago Lith. Co.	20×24½
1025	Boscobel 1869		Ruger & Stoner, Madison, Wisconsin	Chicago Lith. Co.	21×22½
1026	Chippewa-Falls 1886	H. W. [H. Wellge]	Norris, Wellge & Co., Milwaukee, Wisconsin	Beck & Pauli, Lith., Milwaukee, Wisconsin	22×26½
1027	Chippewa-Falls 1907	H. W. [H. Wellge]	H. Wellge, Milwaukee, Wis.		20×30½
1028	Columbus 1868	A. Ruger		Chicago Lith. Co.	20×24
1029	Delavan 1884	H. Brosius	J. J. Stoner, Madison, Wisconsin	Beck & Pauli, Milwaukee, Wisconsin	17½×27½
1030	Fond DuLac 1867	A. Ruger		Chicago Lith. Co.	22×28½
1031	Fort Atkinson 1870	[Albert Ruger]	Ruger & Stoner, Madison, Wisconsin	Merchant's Lith. Co., Chicago	17½×20½
1032	Green Bay & Fort Howard 1867	A. Ruger		Chicago Lith. Co.	22×28
1033	Hudson 1870	[Albert Ruger]	Ruger & Stoner, Madison, Wisconsin	Merchant's Lith. Co., Chicago	20½×23

No.	City and Date	Artist	Publisher	Lithographer or Printer	Map Size (Inches)
1034	Hurley 1886		Norris, Wellge & Co., Milwaukee, Wisconsin	Beck & Pauli, Lith., Milwaukee, Wisconsin	12½×19
1035	Jefferson 1870		Ruger & Stoner, Madison, Wisconsin	Chicago Lith. Co.	20½×23
1036	La Crosse 1867	A. Ruger		Chicago Lith. Co.	23×28½
1037	La Crosse 1873	Geo. H. Ellsbury		Milwaukee Lith. & Eng. Co.	14×23¼
1038	La Crosse 1887		H. Wellge, Milwaukee, Wisconsin	Beck & Pauli, Lith., Milwaukee, Wisconsin	23×41
1039	Madison 1867	A. Ruger		Chicago Lith. Co., Chicago	21¼×28¼
1040	Madison 1885		Norris, Wellge & Co., Milwaukee, Wisconsin	Beck & Pauli, Lith., Milwaukee, Wisconsin	22×31½
1041	Madison 1885		Norris, Wellge & Co., Milwaukee		27½×41½
1042	Medford 1885	H. Wellge	Norris, Wellge & Co., Milwaukee, Wisconsin	Beck & Pauli, **Lith.**, **Milwaukee**, Wisconsin	15×18½
1043	Menomonee Falls 1886		Norris, Wellge & Co., Milwaukee, Wisconsin	Beck & Pauli, Lith., Milwaukee, Wisconsin	12×18½
1044	Merrill 1883	H. Wellge	J. J. Stoner, Madison, Wisconsin	Beck & Pauli, Lith., Milwaukee, Wisconsin	13½×31
1045	Milwaukee [ca. 1872]	H. H. Bailey	Holzapfel & Eskuche, Milwaukee, Wisconsin	Milwaukee Lith. & Eng. Co.	27×39
1046	Milwaukee 1879		J. J. Stoner & Co., Madison, Wisconsin	Beck & Pauli, Lith., Milwaukee, Wisconsin	26½×39
1047	Milwaukee 1882		Beck & Pauli, Milwaukee, Wisconsin		16½×27
1048	Oconomowoc 1885	H. Wellge	Norris, Wellge & Co., Milwaukee, Wisconsin	Beck & Pauli, Lith., Milwaukee, Wisconsin	20×30½
1049	Oshkosh 1867	A. Ruger		Chicago Lith. Co.	22½×28¼
1050	Portage 1868	A. Ruger		Chicago Lith. Co.	22½×28

No.	City and Date	Artist	Publisher	Lithographer or Printer	Map Size (Inches)
1051	Prairie Du Chien 1870	[Albert Ruger]	Ruger & Stoner, Madison, Wisconsin	Chicago Lith. Co.	21×23½
1052	Prairie Du Sac 1870	[Albert Ruger]	Ruger & Stoner, Madison, Wisconsin	Chicago Lith. Co.	16×17
1053	Racine 1883 (Inset Racine 1841)		J. J. Stoner, Madison, Wisconsin		23×34
1054	Reedsburg 1874		J. J. Stoner, Madison, Wisconsin	J. Knauber & Co., Milwaukee, Wisconsin	15×16½
1055	Ripon 1867	A. Ruger		Chicago Lith. Co.	21×24
1056	Sauk City 1870	[Albert Ruger]	Ruger & Stoner, Madison, Wisconsin	Chicago Lith. Co.	15×18½
1057	Sheboygan 1885	H. Wellge	Norris, Wellge & Co., Milwaukee, Wisconsin	Beck & Pauli, Lith., Milwaukee, Wisconsin	22½×31
1058	Superior 1883	H. Wellge	J. J. Stoner, Madison, Wisconsin	Beck & Pauli, Lith., Milwaukee, Wisconsin	13×31½
1059	Superior 1913		Bradley-Brink Co.	Bureau of Engraving, Minneapolis	21×27½
1060	Superior, Wisconsin & Duluth, Minnesota 1915	H. Wellge; Russell		Freeman Eng. Co., Minneapolis	16½×35½
1061	Washburn 1886		Norris, Wellge & Co., Milwaukee, Wisconsin	Beck & Pauli, Milwaukee, Wisconsin	16×20½
1062	Watertown 1867	A. Ruger		Chicago Lith. Co.	22½×28½
1063	Watertown 1885	H. Wellge	Norris, Wellge & Co., Milwaukee, Wisconsin	Beck & Pauli, Milwaukee, Wisconsin	23×31½
1064	Waukesha 1880	H. Wellge	J. J. Stoner, Madison, Wisconsin	Beck & Pauli, Lith., Milwaukee, Wisconsin	20×26
1065	Wauwatosa & Western Suburbs of Milwaukee 1892		Marr & Richard Engraving Co., Milwaukee		20×29

No.	City and Date	Artist	Publisher	Lithographer or Printer	Map Size (Inches)
1066	West Superior 1887	Henry Wellge & Co., Milwaukee, Wis.	A. L. Langellier		18×21½
1067	Whitewater 1885		Norris, Wellge & Co., Milwaukee, Wisconsin	Beck & Pauli, Lith., Milwaukee, Wisconsin	19½×31

Wyoming

1068	Cheyenne 1882	J. J. Stoner	J. J. Stoner, Madison, Wisconsin	Beck & Pauli, Lith., Milwaukee, Wisconsin	17¾×23½

Canada

1069	Brantford, Ontario 1875	H. Brosius		Chas. Shober & Co., Chicago Lith. Co.	23×32
1070	Chatham, Ontario [1870–1880?]				29×39
1071	Halifax, Nova Scotia 1879	A. Ruger			16½×35½
1072	London, Ontario 1872	E. S. Glover	Reproduced for Smallman & Ingram, Ltd. in 1932		15×25½
1072A	Ottawa, Ontario 1876	Herm. Brosius	Reproduced by Canada. Department of Energy, Mines & Resources 1969	Charles Shober & Co., Chicago Lith. Co.	20½×26 photostat
1073	Ottawa, Ontario 1895			Toronto Lithographing Co.	33×42
1074	St. Thomas, Ontario 1895	H. Brosius	J. J. Stoner, Madison, Wis.	C. H. Vogt, Lith.; J. Knauber & Co., Milwaukee	22×32
1075	Victoria, British Columbia 1860	H. O. Tiedemann	Day & Son	T. Picken	10×35
1076	Victoria, British Columbia 1878	E. S. Glover	M. W. Waitt & Co., Victoria, B.C.	A. L. Bancroft & Co., San Francisco, Calif.	23×35½

No.	City and Date	Artist	Publisher	Lithographer or Printer	Map Size (Inches)
1077	Victoria, British Columbia 1889	R. H. ?	Ellis & Co., Victoria, B.C.		27×40
1078	Winnipeg, Manitoba 1880	T. M. Fowler	J. J. Stoner, Madison, Wisc.	Beck & Pauli, Lith., Milwaukee, Wis.	11×16½ photostat
1079	Winnipeg, Manitoba 1881	T. M. Fowler		A. Mortimer Lith. Ottawa	11×16½ photostat

Numbers refer to entries.

☆ U.S. GOVERNMENT PRINTING OFFICE: 1974 O—498-354